On Call

D1292983

BV
3625
·G3
T565x
1991
C2

25030446

On Call

David C. Thompson, MD

WingSpread Publishers
Camp Hill, Pennsylvania

WingSpread Publishers

3825 Hartzdale Drive · Camp Hill, PA 17011
www.wingspreadpublishers.com

A division of Zur Ltd.

On Call
ISBN: 978-1-60066-038-2
LOC Control Number: 2006936035
© 1991 by Zur Ltd.

Previously published by Christian Publications, Inc.
First Christian Publications Edition 1991
First WingSpread Publishers Edition 2006

All rights reserved
Printed in the United States of America

10   09   08   07   5   4   3   2

Unless otherwise indicated,
Scripture taken from the HOLY BIBLE:
NEW INTERNATIONAL VERSION.
Copyright © 1973, 1978, 1984 by the
International Bible Society.
Used by permission of
Zondervan Bible Publishers.

Cover illustration © 1991 by Karl Foster

*I dedicate this book in memory
of Ed and Ruth Thompson.
Their shining example taught me
how to trust in God.*

Contents

Foreword

DAVE AND I BECAME ACQUAINTED during the first days at the Dalat School for Missionary Children in Vietnam. I didn't realize then that some day he would be my son-in-law.

I've followed with interest Dave's determination to be a medical missionary even after the tragic days of the Tet Offensive that claimed the lives of his parents in Banmethuot, Vietnam.

I've known too of his struggles to find the helpmate God had for him.

Aware of the money that can be made in the medical profession in America, Dave had to make a choice. I'm thankful that he made the right one—that God's love compelled him and his family to turn their backs on the so-called "good life" to go to the needy in other lands—to heal their diseases, to turn them from darkness to light, to give them hope. A greater joy and satisfaction money can never buy.

On Call vividly portrays the beautiful way God has worked to draw Dave closer to Himself, to teach him valuable lessons in faith and trust. This is a testimony of answered prayer.

Betty Mitchell
Former missionary to Vietnam

Preface

For years I have shared with others the wonderful things God has done in my life. But I have resisted writing a book because of fear it might result in bringing more attention to myself than to the Lord Jesus Christ whom I serve. I share this biblical sentiment: "Not to us, O LORD, not to us but to your name be the glory, because of your love and faithfulness" (Psalm 115:1).

I have hesitated to write for other reasons as well. Compared to a "glamorous" missionary doctor, the missionary who translates the scriptures or who establishes new churches is all too often seen as dull and one-dimensional. It is a false picture. Medical missions is not the best or only way to bring the world to Christ. It is only one of many exciting methods God is using and it is most effective as part of an overall effort to evangelize a nation.

The matter of putting my story on paper was finally settled in my heart one day when I read: "Come and listen, all you who fear God; let me tell you what he has done for me" (Psalm 66:16). Telling you what He has done for me is what this book is all about.

I do not want this book to encourage anyone who does not really love the business of caring for the sick to become a doctor or nurse in order to become a missionary. Medicine can be a very demanding taskmaster and the moral obligation to use one's knowledge and ability to treat ever-present needs can become a heavy burden indeed. Nevertheless, missionary medicine is where it's at for me!

All of the stories in this book are factual and true. In describing events recounted by others, I sometimes ascribe thoughts to characters and add descriptive details to flesh out and explain subsequent actions and emotions. These are based on what I know about the individuals' personalities, the culture, and the setting.

It is my prayer that God will use this account to encourage others to trust Him so fully that they will be able to serve the Lord Jesus Christ without fear, and in so doing to bring the world to worship at His feet.

David C. Thompson, MD
January, 1990

Introduction

After serving in Africa for four years, I returned to the United States in 1981 to complete a residency in General Surgery. As my training drew to a close, several of my friends asked me if it was not hard to leave the comforts and security of the United States to return to Africa. This was my answer.

The beeping of heart monitors, the swooshing of respirators, the whir of air-conditioning and the murmuring voices of hovering nurses, doctors, technicians, therapists, chaplains and visiting family members fill the fluorescent-lit room. Machines, computers and gadgets of every description hum through mind-numbing calculations and bleep their electronic conclusions in red and green digits above, beside and behind the limp figures lying in all-electric, motorized beds. I am a doctor in the Intensive Care Unit and my patient lingers between life and death. I give orders and nurses add this and turn down that; they twist knobs on a machine crowded with dials, wires, tubes and blinking lights. It breathes for my patient. I write it all down in case I get sued. The patient improves. The thread by which his life hangs becomes a string,

1

a rope, and finally his life seems secure. He will live another year or 10.

My mind sees another place, another time. The face of an African mother as she holds her youngest son in her arms. His disease is steadily paralyzing him. The trust in her eyes moves me, but all my efforts to save the child amount to nothing. He weakens by the day. There are no digital monitors in his room recording the numbers of his slow demise. The thread by which his life hangs unravels, but he and his mother do not complain about my impotence. He is unafraid of death, but still wanting to live. He and his mother talk freely of the kingdom to which he is soon going. She prays to Jesus and weeps for her son every night. My meager medical resources at an end, I entrust mother and child to God.

A monitor alarm buzzes next to me and for a moment I return to the ICU and gaze at the heartbeats registering like neon waves across the screen.

I remember driving the dusty African road back to the boy's home. His mother supports his emaciated body in her arms as we bounce and sway on the rutty road, a fine layer of red dust settling over everything. The heat is stifling. My battered truck breaks down and we cannot go on. The mother walks slowly toward a nearby house with the boy draped across her shoulders. He is unconscious now and his legs swing grotesquely as she staggers through the darkened doorway. He will die in a stranger's home, on a dirt floor, unwashed, clothed in rags—but loved by his mother, his God and me.

I look down at the chart in my hands that has every breath and beat and degree neatly recorded. I return the stares of the microchip wonders with the metallic faces and winking eyes. But my heart is not here. It remains in a dark land, in a dark hut, where an African mother sits holding her dead child in her arms, weeping tears of hope.

1

The Heritage

It is 1932 in French Indochina (now known as Southeast Asia). A lone American drives through a small Cambodian village that straddles the road. He is weary and although he knows no one in the village, he stops. Perhaps the village chief will offer him a place to sleep. He hopes that at least he will be accorded the same respect as the French rulers.

He parks in front of a prominent house standing on eight foot high mahogany pillars. A crowd of curious villagers immediately gathers and the village chief soon appears from another house. The stranger introduces himself as a protestant missionary. The chief seems honored to be able to comply with the request for a night's lodging and invites the missionary to eat with him.

The missionary's arrival is an exciting event in the life of the village of Kabal Chua and after supper people crowd around the chief's house. The missionary is granted permission to speak

and haltingly tells his rapt listeners the most
amazing story they have ever heard, the story of
the Creator-God. They are surprised to learn
that this God is interested in them. Their
amazement grows as the pale man tells how the
Creator's Son, Jesus, came to earth, how He
performed great miracles and healed the sick,
how He invited the people of the world to turn
from evil to serve and obey the Creator who
loved them.

The Creator's Son is so very different from the
lord Buddha. The listeners shake their heads in
dismay when the missionary relates that despite
the miracles Jesus performed, the people did not
believe He came from the Creator. They are
shocked when he tells them how some turned
against Jesus, rejected His message and then
killed Him on a cross. When he tells how this Jesus
was buried, then rose from the grave three days
later, their amazement fades into doubt. How
could someone rise from the dead, even if He was
the Son of the Creator-God? Perhaps He never
really died. Had lord Buddha not taught that
when a person dies he will live again as an animal
or even as an insect, depending on how he has
lived his life?

And what's more, says the missionary, this Jesus
told His followers that if they believed in Him and
obeyed His teachings, they would live with Him
forever in a paradise. The crowd is polite but skeptical as the missionary recounts how Jesus as-
cended from the earth into heaven, promising

someday to return. The people thank him for the interesting story. But the missionary is not finished.

"This Jesus has sent me here to tell you this good news. If you wish to follow Him, stay and talk with me." They quickly cover their embarrassed smiles. Nobody would do anything so foolish. They can hardly wait to leave so they can talk and laugh among themselves. All leave—except one.

Both the missionary and the chief are surprised. The young man's name is Lop. He is about 20 years old. Hesitantly he asks the missionary to explain more about the story he has just heard. They talk for several hours. It is very late when Lop bows his head and prays a simple prayer. He asks God to forgive him for the evil he has done in his life; he acknowledges that Jesus is the true Son of the Creator-God; he vows to obey His teachings. Lop promises to come by in the morning.

The missionary is up early and after a breakfast of rice and fish begins packing his car. Lop is walking towards him, a wide smile on his young face. They sit down on a fallen tree trunk to talk. Lop wants to know when the missionary will be back. With a heavy heart, the missionary tells him he doesn't know. But he promises to stop and see Lop if he ever passes through Kabal Chua again. And he promises to pray for Lop. That is all he can do.

Anxiety and sadness cloud Lop's eyes. How can he follow Jesus if he doesn't know what to do? The missionary responds gently but firmly: "Lop, you must pray to Jesus every day and you must ask Him to help you. He will hear you and He will show you what to do and what not to do. And you must do one more thing—you must ask Jesus to send someone to you who can teach your people about Jesus." Lop looks down at his calloused hands. He has decided to follow this Jesus, the Son of the Creator-God, but he will be the only believer in his village.

It is difficult for the missionary to leave but there are so many others waiting for him. He is responsible for them, too. The Lord will have to take care of Lop and the village of Kabal Chua.

At planting time Lop did not participate in the animal sacrifices to appease the spirits and at harvest time he did not celebrate the traditional ceremonies and festivals to thank lord Buddha for his benevolence. His refusal shocked the entire village, because in their view his unreasonable behavior was endangering them all. The religious leaders and village elders tried to reason with him, but Lop refused to change or to stop praying to Jesus. Various social measures were taken to punish and isolate him. When social pressures did not work, the religious leaders invoked the spirits to cause him harm, even to kill him. Yet Lop continued to pray daily to the Creator-God and to His Son, asking Him to send someone to teach him and his people how to follow Jesus.

As Lop prayed, a seven-year-old boy named Carl was growing up on a farm in western Pennsylvania. His coal-miner father was an alcoholic. When the boy was four years old, his father drove home from a tavern and in an alcoholic haze ran over and killed a child. He was put in jail and, while awaiting trial, hanged himself in his cell. Carl was one of his two surviving children.

Times were hard and Carl's mother remarried hastily. Within weeks she knew she had made a great mistake. Her new husband took a particular dislike to Carl. When the boy was disobedient, he beat him brutally. More times than he could remember his mother had to pour hot water on his back in the mornings to free the bedsheets from his wounds. Once, because he was holding his fork incorrectly, his stepfather punched him in the face so forcefully that he fell backwards in his chair and down the cellar stairs. Though Carl's face was bleeding, his stepfather insisted he resume his place at the table and hold his fork correctly. Not surprisingly, the boy grew to hate his stepfather.

One day Carl's mother went into the nearby town of New Kensington to shop and to visit friends. Passing by the doors of a Christian and Missionary Alliance church, she heard singing that stirred childhood memories in her battered heart. She turned and entered the church. That day she met Jesus Christ.

The change in her life was breathtaking. The entire family was surprised that she no longer re-

sponded angrily to her husband's insults. Later
that week, when he got drunk and made fun of her
newfound faith, she answered him gently. When
he got angry and struck her, she did not hit back.

Carl, now 16 years old, noticed the change and
when he asked her why she was so different, she
told him she had given her life to Christ. He asked
to go with her to church the following Sunday. His
stepfather was not pleased, but allowed the two of
them to go. The pastor talked about Jesus Christ,
about sin, about hell and heaven. When he invited
the congregation to follow Jesus, Carl went forward weeping. He and his mother returned home
rejoicing, but their happiness and joy only served
to further enrage his stepfather. As Carl tried to
explain his newfound faith, his stepfather turned
white with anger, snatched a shotgun from over
the fireplace and, pointing the loaded gun at Carl,
ordered him to leave the house and never come
back. Carl had no choice but to walk out the door.
He never lived in his mother's house again.

Carl found lodging in someone's attic in New
Kensington. He worked part-time and attended
the church where he had met Christ. The
church people provided the love he had missed
all of his young life.

One day a missionary came to the church and
told about the people of Asia waiting to hear
about Christ. God spoke to Carl and he announced his intention to become a missionary.
After training at Nyack Missionary Training In-
stitute, he, along with his new bride, pastored a

church in western Pennsylvania. In 1948 they sailed from New York to Cambodia.

Carl and his wife were appointed to plant a church in the provincial capital of Kratie, in eastern Cambodia. The governor, however, was a strong Buddhist and forbade them to evangelize or establish a church in the town. Instead, they began visiting the villages surrounding the town, preaching the gospel and hoping to plant at least one church. One day they drove into the little village of Kabal Chua.

The Cambodians were fascinated to see not only a white man but his white wife and two small white children. They marveled at the children's blond hair, fair skin, freckles and blue eyes. The missionaries set up a flannel-covered board on the hood of their Jeep. Although Carl spoke with a strange accent and made funny mistakes, the village chief agreed to let him speak to the crowd.

It had been about 18 years since Lop had chosen to follow Jesus Christ. He had suffered greatly for his decision, but had not turned back. He had even won a grudging respect from the villagers.

The crowd in the center of the village attracted Lop's attention. His heart stirred when he saw the tall white man. Could this be . . . ? He was afraid to finish the thought. He had been disappointed so many times before and now he hardly dared hope. Probably it was just another Frenchman.

He was surprised to hear the man speaking Cambodian. Lop listened intently, caught up in the story and intrigued by the pictures the white woman placed on the board on the Jeep. At the mention of the Creator-God, Lop felt his heart jump in his chest. Could it really be? He had to be sure. The white woman put a picture of a baby on the board. There were strangely-dressed people kneeling in a circle around the baby, bowing to him, with cows looking over their shoulders. The white man said the baby was the Creator-God's Son, Jesus.

In an instant, Lop jumped up and began shouting. "You've come! You've come! You've come for me!" There were tears in his eyes, but he didn't care. He was too happy to care. The Creator-God had answered his prayers!

I marvel at this story even today. God took an abused and unloved child, an outcast teenager from an unchurched, violence-filled, indigent home and took him around the world to teach Lop and his people about Jesus. Lop became the head elder of the church that was established in Kabal Chua. His testimony served to win many to Christ. He served God faithfully and joyfully until 1975, when the Khmer Rouge swept over the land, killing Lop and all who were known to be Christians.

I write this story as I heard it from Carl's own lips. Carl Edward Thompson was my father. I was one of the white children in Kabal Chua the day Lop's prayer was so dramatically answered. Carl's wife, my mother, was Ruth Stebbins, whose father and mother were pioneer missionaries to Vietnam. My mother's mother grew up in the West Indies, the child of missionary parents. I am the fourth generation of my family to serve God as a missionary.

2

The Telephone Call

The college cafeteria was still nearly empty at 7 a.m. on that wintry morning in February, 1968. I had just begun to eat breakfast when another student hurried into the cafeteria to tell me that there was an urgent, long-distance telephone call in the Dean's office, and that the Dean was holding the line open. I left my tray and hurried to his office, trying to imagine who might be calling me at this time of morning. A chill of premonition went through me as I climbed the steps and entered the building.

There were six or eight faculty and staff members in the room. The Dean greeted me solemnly and showed me to the phone. My heart was pounding. I wondered if the others could hear it.

"Hello?"

"Hello, David? Is that you?"

"Yes."

"David, this is headquarters in New York. I don't know how to tell you this, but there has been heavy fighting in Vietnam over the Tet holidays. We have just received news that your mother and father have been killed by the communist forces." There was a pause. "David, we're all shocked and so sorry."

A hundred thousand images flashed through my mind, stopping finally at the last day I saw my parents alive.

It was a warm, summer morning in Nyack, New York as we stood outside our rented home and said goodbye. I had to leave for work. Since Cambodia had closed to all missionaries, my folks had agreed to go as missionaries to South Vietnam. Their flight that day would take them to Saigon. There were tears in our eyes as we hugged each other.

"Goodbye, Mom, Dad. I'll be praying for you that you'll be safe."

"We'll be praying for you, David," Mom said. Dad was strangely quiet for a moment, his eyes misted with tears.

"You may never see us again." His words seemed overly dramatic. "No matter what happens, son, I want you to follow after Jesus."

I disliked mushy farewells and this was turning into one. I smiled and hugged them again, my eyes dry, my heart unsuspecting.

"I'll be fine. You be careful!" I turned and walked away. At the top of the bank I glanced back, waving to them once more. They stood together, tears in their eyes, just looking at me. Finally they waved back.

The rest of the telephone conversation, even the rest of that day, remains shrouded in a kind of gray mist. I walked alone across the campus to my room and locked the door. I wept on my knees for what seemed like hours, but was probably less than 45 minutes. All the while, a single word filled my mind: Why? When there was no answer, a kind of rage began to grow in my heart. Why, God, why did you let this happen? In reply—only the silence of an empty room.

Why don't you answer me, God? Don't you care about how I feel? Why won't you tell me why you let both my parents be killed now? If you made the worlds, why can't you give me an answer so I can understand why this happened? It was as though He did not want to answer. In the silence I struggled to understand a God who had saved my parents from death on previous occasions. What had they done wrong to deserve death this time?

I remembered how God had intervened when Mom and Dad had first gone to eastern Cambodia during the French-Indochina War. The roads were mined and cars were often ambushed by the nationalist rebels. The Mission had assigned them to Kratie, but there was no safe way to get there. The French military authorities discouraged them from even attempting to drive, but when they saw that my father was determined to go, they counseled him to wait for a military convoy. Dad felt this was just as dangerous as traveling alone and told the French commandant that he preferred to travel by himself. God had sent them to Cambodia and if God wanted them to preach the gospel in Kratie He would have to protect them on the way.

The French commander was appalled that Dad would even contemplate such a risk. Didn't the Reverend Thompson know that the rebels had skewered French children on upright poles as a warning to foreigners to get out of their country? Did the Reverend think that he looked any different than a Frenchman? But Dad was not to be deterred. Reluctantly, the commander agreed to let them travel alone. He advised Dad to drive as fast as the roads permitted and warned him not to stop under any circumstances—an invitation for ambush, he said.

I was too small to remember the trip but I heard the story many times from my mother. She told how Dad drove at breakneck speed and finally broke a spring on the rough road. While Mother desperately prayed for our safety, he stopped the Jeep to survey the damage. A French army truck full of troops came up behind us. For a wonderful moment we thought that the Lord had sent the troops along to protect us, but to our dismay, the truck swept on by in a cloud of dust. One hundred yards down the road, the truck hit a land mine and overturned. While we watched in horror, rebels hiding in the bushes poured gunfire into the burning wreckage, killing everyone. Had God not stopped our car with a broken spring, we would have been the victims.

The second time God spared Dad and Mom
was even more dramatic. Dad told the story pub-
licly so many times that I know it by heart. We had
been in Kratie for perhaps a year. French troops
were garrisoned in the city because it was a provincial capital. One day the French commander
received secret information that a large force of
rebels was going to attack the French rubber plan-
tations outside of the town of Snoul, 80 kilometers
away. Confident that his information was correct,
the commander loaded his troops on trucks and
raced to Snoul, hoping to surprise the rebels. The
purported attack never materialized. It was a rebel
trick.

The actual plan was for a rebel force of about
2,000 to attack Kratie where we lived. As dusk
fell, a soldier knocked on our door and asked if
we would like to come to the hotel where they
were planning to fight to the finish. Father
thanked him, but said no. Instead, he said, he
and his wife would pray. God had not brought
them to Kratie to be destroyed before they had
done the work they were sent to do.

I remember having to stay under the bed with
my sister while Dad and Mom knelt and prayed.
Mom said we were very fussy and made it hard
for them to pray. As Dad told it, around two
a.m. a white flare lit up the square between our
house and the hotel. The attack on the hotel
started soon after.

Bullets flew everywhere. Suddenly, a red flare
shot up and burned briefly in the night sky. The

shooting tapered off. In the morning there was no sign of the rebels and nobody understood why the rebels had abandoned the attack. The French commander returned later that day from Snoul and was surprised to find the city intact. In 1955 the French granted independence to Cambodia, returning power to the king of Cambodia. The king promised amnesty to all the rebels who would turn in their weapons and pledge allegiance to him—some of the rebels were communists. On the announced day, the provincial rebels came by the thousands to the town square and stacked their weapons in a great pile. There were speeches and ceremonies all day. Towards the middle of the day, the retiring French commander asked Dad to translate for him while he spoke to the rebel commander. After the introductions, the commander asked the rebel leader, "Why did you not take the city the night we were diverted to Snoul, leaving Kratie defenseless?"

The rebel commander seemed surprised by the question. He remembered the night very well, he said, and suggested that the French commander was mistaken, for when the rebels attacked Kratie they were confronted by thousands of French soldiers. There were troops everywhere—more than he had seen at any other time during the war! Since his rebel force numbered only 2,000 men, they had decided to flee.

With Dad interpreting, the French commander and the rebel leader argued about the events of that night. Only Dad understood what had happened: the army of the Lord had saved us. God's angels had appeared as French soldiers in such great numbers that the rebels withdrew.

As I wept alone in my college room, I heard God speak to me for the first time in my life. Although I did not hear a voice or audible words, I knew and understood what He was saying to me.

"David, do you trust Me?"

What did that have to do with anything, I wondered. Of course, I trusted Him! Didn't He know that I had given my life to Him and followed His ways obediently from the time I was five years old? Even as a child, had I not trustingly invited Him to live in my heart? As I waited, He spoke again.

"David, do you trust Me?"

What was I supposed to answer? I had already dedicated myself to serve Him as a missionary doctor.

I remembered that day, too. I was 14 years old, traveling in Cambodia with our family, riding in the back of the Land Rover. We had been driving for about six hours on a pot-holed road when we saw a smashed-up truck ahead. On the opposite side of the road was a bus with the front end damaged. People were scattered along both sides. We stopped the Land Rover and got out. A man informed us that the two vehicles had been approaching each other at high speed. Pointing to a large pothole in the center of the road, he explained that the truck had swerved to miss the pothole and had hit the oncoming bus head-on only minutes before our arrival.

Father knew a little about treating sores and injuries, so he asked if anyone was seriously injured. The man pointed to the bus driver propped up against a nearby mango tree. He was probably going to die, we were told. Father motioned for me to come with him.

A group of onlookers stood around the injured man, watching helplessly as he struggled to breathe. Periodically he coughed up blood. The group parted to let us get closer to him. After hesitating a moment, Father knelt down next to the bus driver and introduced himself in Cambodian. The man nodded in acknowledgment. It was obvious even to me that unless someone did something soon he would die. I knew that there was no hospital within 300 kilometers. While I was away getting the man a drink of water, Father asked him if he felt ready to meet God. The man slowly shook his head. Would he like to know how he could get to heaven, Father persisted. The man looked at Dad for a long time, his chest heaving with every breath. Then he looked at me. Despair filled his eyes as he coughed up a large amount of blood.

"Please, don't talk to me now about your God!" he gasped. "Just help me not to die!" With great sadness Dad looked at him and shook his head.

"I don't know how to help you," he said. The man took several more swallows of water and turned his head away. Father motioned for me to come back to the car. We walked in silence, aware that the man would not last more than a few minutes and knowing that without Christ he would spend eternity in hell.

The rest of the trip I said very little, reliving the entire experience. Over and over I heard the man's desperate pleas and felt again our helplessness. If only we could have helped him to live, perhaps he would have listened to us and perhaps he would have received Christ. The more I thought about it, the more I knew what I wanted to do with my life. I wanted to help the sick people of the world who had no one to help them so that, unlike this man, they would live to hear about Christ's love and believe in Him. By the time we reached Pnom Penh I had solemnly promised God that I would devote my life to that task.

That was why now on this cold February morning in 1968 I was a pre-med student at Geneva College in Beaver Falls, Pennsylvania.

One further question remained in my mind: What would happen to my brothers and sisters? At 19, I was the oldest son. My sister Judy was one year older than I, but Dale was 16, Laurel was 11 and Tom was only eight. I understood that they had left Banmethuot for the Mission boarding school in Malaysia only three days before the attack and were safe. Who would care for them now? Who would help them to understand why they could never go home again? I could not even talk to them, let alone comfort them as an older brother. What about it, Lord? How about some answers?

God answered me, but it was not what I wanted to hear. For the third time, He asked, "David, do you trust Me?" I understood what it was He wanted from me. It was impossible; it was heartless; it was unfair! How could God ask such a thing of anyone? I could not do what He asked. I would not! My mind, my emotions, my spirit rebelled. God wanted me to thank Him. No, I could never, never thank Him that my parents were lost to me. He was asking for the ultimate expression of my trust.

There followed a great struggle in my heart. On the one hand I loved God and wanted to please Him in everything, but on the other hand, I was heartbroken over the loss of the two most precious people in my life. I could not conceive of any good coming out of their death. They had been in their mid 40s, at the peak of their effectiveness as missionaries. They had just learned Vietnamese, their fifth language, after English, French, Cambodian and Hmong. How did that make sense? Yet I knew that I did not have to understand God's ways to accept them. I knew that if I did not surrender, I could not go on walking with the Lord in the same way as before.

There were many people praying for me that day. No doubt it was their prayers that brought me to the place where I finally surrendered. "Lord, I do not understand and I don't feel any real thankfulness in my heart for what You allowed to happen to my parents and me. But because You ask, because I trust You, because I

love You and because I know You really love me,
I will thank You for letting this happen."

Those were the hardest words I had ever spoken. Not really expecting anything to happen, I
was surprised to feel peace pouring over my soul
like a healing balm. To my amazement, the turmoil that moments before was tearing my heart
apart began to abate. Something supernatural
was happening. My parents were still dead. I
was still alone in my room. My brothers and sisters and I were still orphaned and separated by
oceans. But in my heart was a feeling that I can
only describe as restful.

I got up off my knees and packed my bag to go
to my sister in New York. Pastor L.R. Van Horn
of the Beaver Falls Alliance Church bought me
a ticket and got me on the train. Judy was waiting at the station, but even as we fell into each
other's arms and wept, the turmoil did not dis-
place the sense of God's peace. After just three
days I returned to Geneva College.

It was some time until I was told how brutally
my mother and father had died. I learned that
they had been shaken from their sleep in the
early morning hours when North Vietnamese
infiltrators blew up Carolyn Griswold's house
next door. In the dark, with firing all around,
Mom and Dad had heard her cries but had been
unable to rescue her. In the light of day, they
discovered that her father too had been crushed
in the wreckage.

Two days later, as the battle for the city of Banmethuot raged around them, Mom and Dad huddled in a neighboring missionary's house. North Vietnamese soldiers entered their house and blew it up. Realizing they were no longer safe in any of the houses, they all took refuge in a bunker hastily dug in what had been the trash pit.

When the North Vietnamese finally took the city of Banmethuot, they did not permit my parents nor the other missionaries with them to surrender. Instead, they cruelly mowed them down with machine gun fire. As Mom crouched and Dad stood in a bunker behind the mission house, his hands in the air, the North Vietnamese finished them off with hand grenades. Only one missionary, Mrs. Marie Ziemer, survived to tell the story.

My encounter with God after my parents' death only underscored my need to trust God with the people and things that were most precious to me. I had already learned through experience that God was trustworthy by the dramatic way in which He had provided for me to go to Geneva College.

3

The Miracle

A friend studying pre-med at Geneva College spoke so enthusiastically about the school that I decided to apply. I was accepted into the freshman class of 1966. Quite naive about college and thinking I would have to get top grades before I could even qualify for a scholarship, I did not apply for any student aid before arriving.

The Mission promised a monthly allowance which at that time amounted to a little over $100. All of my assets combined did not amount to even one-fourth of the expected annual expenses. Nevertheless, remembering Mother's statement that if God wanted me to become a missionary doctor He would provide the money, I believed that He would supply, although I didn't know how.

The seriousness of what I was expecting God to do did not really dawn on me until registration day. I found my way down to the school gymnasium where registration tables were set up. All went well until I arrived at the cashier. She took my registration card and after ringing up all the courses I was signed up for and adding my room and board, she announced that my bill for the first semester was several thousand dollars. I was prepared for this and handed her $50 that my dad's brother had given me. The cashier was not impressed, particularly since I had no loans, grants or scholarships lined up to cover even half of the fees. She directed me to another table where a nice lady from the finance office asked me how I intended to pay my bill.

With some hesitation I explained that I was expecting God to provide the money. Her mouth did not drop open but it might as well have. She got up, walked toward a serious-looking man in a dark suit and pointing back at me, handed him the bill. My six foot three inches felt like only three inches as he motioned for me to come over. He introduced himself as the Dean of Finance and asked what arrangements I had made to pay for my first semester. This time I remembered to mention that I was planning to work part-time. I told him that I was trusting God to provide the rest. He seemed sympathetic, but said that I would have to come talk with him in his office later in the week and that perhaps I would have to take out some loans. My heart sank at the word. How could I pay back school loans on a missionary salary?

Classes started the next day and that same day I began looking for work. I didn't know anyone in Beaver Falls and I didn't even know where to look for work. Besides, I didn't have a car, so getting work in town was not a practical option. Having grown up in Asia, I knew how to work, but I didn't know how one went about finding a job. My first job in America had been helping a neighbor build a retaining wall behind his house. He outlined how he wanted the bank dug out and the dirt moved elsewhere and how he wanted railroad ties stacked to hold up the bank. I worked alone 10 hours a day, digging dirt and hauling it away in a wheelbarrow. During the second week it began to drizzle. In Cambodia, men didn't stop working unless it rained heavily and this was only a typical North American all-day drizzle. As the day wore on, the ground turned to mud and I became thoroughly drenched. Although the rain and mud made the work more difficult, I carried on and thought little of it. When my employer returned home and saw me, he was speechless. Didn't I know not to come to work on a rainy day?

The second week at Geneva I learned that the college was looking for someone to clean the bathrooms in the men's dormitory. The pay was one dollar an hour. I signed up immediately, wondering why no one else seemed interested. I soon learned that cleaning toilets was not a job to dawdle over. I became so expert that I usually got the job done in under an hour. That meant that I was earning less than a dollar a day. I soon realized that I would never pay my way through college cleaning toilets!

The second week of school the director of the college's sixty-voice acapella touring choir announced tryouts. My roommate, David MacMillan, had a rich baritone voice and he was accepted immediately. He urged me to join too. The idea appealed to me. I had enjoyed choir in both high school and church and although my tenor voice was a bit reedy, I was better than average at reading music and I could harmonize. I determined to try out the following Monday. Just to be sure that I would get in the choir, I began praying about it.

On Sunday I came down with a cold. By Monday morning I could hardly talk. I was irritated that the Lord had not kept me from getting a cold at such an important time in my life. Perhaps the Lord would make the choir director understand. Supremely confident that God was smoothing the way in response to my prayers, I tried out.

By the time I got to his room, the choir master was tired and grouchy. He asked me what part I sang and when I croaked that I sang tenor, he handed me a hymnal opened to a song he had selected. I started to explain to him that I couldn't sing because I had laryngitis, but he glared at me over the top of the piano and ordered, "Sing!" When he'd heard about ten seconds worth, he stopped playing, thanked me, and, brushing aside my efforts to explain, called for the next student. The following day my name did not appear on the list of those accepted. I was angry at the Lord. Hadn't I prayed about it? That was always sup-

posed to work. Yet He had done nothing to help
me. It seemed to me that God had botched the
job, but since Christians aren't supposed to think
that way, I tried to forget about the whole thing.

One day I noticed that most of my dormmates
were coming to class in wrinkled shirts. The
Thompson Ironing Service was born. I had never
ironed a shirt in my life but I borrowed an iron and
an ironing board and began ironing for 25 cents a
shirt. It still wasn't enough.

My typing skills were better than average and I
had a good typewriter, so I offered my typing services at 15 cents a page. Corrections were an extra
10 cents a page. Soon I was busy every evening
ironing shirts, typing papers and cleaning toilets.
When those jobs were done, I got down to studying, often until one or two in the morning. The
Dean of Finance hadn't contacted me yet and I
wondered how long it would be before he called
me in for "the discussion." I wasn't about to re-
mind him.

About four weeks into the term, the school ad-
ministration announced that there would be a
freshman talent show. My roommate and I decided to enter. For weeks we worked on a humorous musical skit I wrote in which we acted and
sang. Dave had an evening job cleaning the class-
rooms in a nearby elementary school. As we
mopped the floors together, we practiced. By the
day of the show we had the skit down to perfec-
tion.

There were many good presentations, but our skit was one of the best. We won a prize. As we filed out of the gymnasium, the choir director approached me.

"David, that was a very good skit you two put on!" I looked up, surprised that he would remember my name. I smiled and thanked him.

"You know, you really can sing tenor after all!" Now he had my interest. "I need tenors in the choir and I'd like you to join. How about it?" I sadly explained to him that although I wanted very much to sing in the choir, because I had to work to earn money for school, I didn't have the time. He seemed genuinely disappointed, but not as much as I.

That afternoon I found a note in my mailbox from the Dean of Finance, asking me to come to his office the next morning. My heart sank.

I counted up all of my earnings and found I had about $150. I had spent all of the allowance money from the Mission to buy books. I entered the finance office with a sense of impending doom. The Dean greeted me warmly and got right to the point.

"Well, David, has the Lord provided you with the funds for your first semester at school?"

"Not entirely, sir." I placed my $150 on the desk in front of me. He looked at it briefly, then at my bill.

"Have you considered a school loan?" he asked. I explained to him why I didn't want to take out any loans. He looked at me thoughtfully.

"Mr. Greig talked to me yesterday and it seems he really wants you to sing in his choir."

"Yes, he did ask me to join the choir but I had to refuse because, now that I'm working, I don't have time to sing in the choir three afternoons a week and study too." The Dean nodded and continued nodding, obviously thinking hard.

"Let me ask you this, David," he said finally, making his hands into a steeple. "If we were to find some grants and scholarships to pay for your first semester here in school, would you consider quitting the jobs you have to sing in the choir?" I stared at him, my mouth ajar.

"Do you mean not work and sing in the choir?" I finally asked.

"That's right. Your professors tell me you're an excellent student. If you keep your grades up, I think we might be able to find you other scholarships next semester." I wanted to kiss the man! As I walked out the door, my feet barely touching the ground, I realized I had seriously misjudged the Lord. Actually I realized so many things at once that it took days for me to sort it all out. I remembered a promise that I had learned as a child: "Trust in the Lord with all your heart, and lean not on your own understanding; in all your ways acknowledge him, and he will make your paths straight" (Proverbs 3:5-6).

That night I asked God to forgive me for failing to trust Him.

4

Medical School

After the death of my parents, I decided that although I could no longer dream of working alongside them, I could follow in their footsteps. Life took on a new urgency and I decided to go to summer school in order to graduate from Geneva College in three years instead of four. God continued to provide for my financial needs through a combination of grants, scholarships, speaking honorariums and gifts, particularly from members of the Beaver Falls Alliance Church.

The challenge of getting into medical school seemed almost insurmountable. The collegiate and post-graduate landscape was littered with those who had tried and had been rejected. Then, of course, there was the ever-present problem of finances.

God had certainly provided for me in response to my mother's faith. Now she was gone. Would He do the same in response to my faith? Admittedly filled with doubt, I wrote to six med-

ical schools, all in Pennsylvania. The school I
wanted most to attend was the University of
Pittsburgh School of Medicine. It was considered to be one of the most difficult to get into.
I began filling out applications. All had one
question in common: "Why do you want to become a doctor?" They wanted an essay-type answer, preferably truthful. I was greatly perplexed
by the question. It was not that I didn't know the
answer—I wasn't certain that the truth would be
acceptable. If I wrote that I wanted to become a
doctor because I felt God calling me to become a
medical missionary, they would no doubt laugh
hilariously and throw my application into the
trash.

As I prayed about what to do I remembered
the story of Gideon putting out the fleece. I
sensed the Lord's approval as a plan formed in
my mind. I would divide the six applications into
two piles of three. On one set I would write the
truth, but only part of it. I would say that I
wanted to become a doctor because I loved the
idea of helping sick people get better. On the
other three I would write the same thing but I
would include my call from God. The question
then became, in which pile would I put the application for the University of Pittsburgh?

After much soul-searching and prayer, I put it
in the "whole truth" pile. I committed the matter
to the Lord and mailed the applications. Now all
I had to do was wait for a request for an interview from several or all of them.

I never heard from the three schools in the "part truth" pile; but two of the three schools that knew about my call to become a missionary doctor responded by asking for an interview. One was the University of Pittsburgh. I was to report to the Children's Hospital in Pittsburgh for an interview with Dr. W.B. Kiesewetter, the Chief of Pediatric Surgery.

On the appointed day, I drove to Pittsburgh from Beaver Falls. A sense of panic gripped me as the hour for the appointment approached. It was difficult finding a parking place. When I finally found Dr. Kiesewetter's office, his secretary asked me to be seated and took my file into him. Ten minutes later Dr. Kiesewetter buzzed for me to come in.

Dr. Kiesewetter was a trim, distinguished-looking man, with white hair and reading glasses far down on his nose. He turned, looked over the rims, then stood and shook my hand. His smile was friendly but formal. He asked me to be seated.

"I've been looking over your application, David, and I found it to be somewhat . . . uh . . . unique." I felt my stomach contract. "Tell me, what do you mean by your statement that God has called you to be a doctor?"

I swallowed hard and told him about witnessing a man die when I was a fourteen-year-old in Cambodia and that I felt God had permitted me to see that to call me into missionary medicine.

"How do you know it was God?" he asked.

"Well, He spoke to me in my heart," I explained. It sounded weak and his raised eyebrow confirmed it.

"How? Did you hear His voice?"

"Uh . . . no. He just spoke to me in my . . . uh . . . heart and I knew that He wanted me to do that." Although it was March and the room was cool I felt sweat trickling down my ribs under my white shirt. He nodded skeptically and turned back to the application.

"If you become a doctor, then, you're going to preach to people?"

"Well, I want to share my faith in Jesus Christ with them if I can," I explained, trying to stifle feelings of despair at the way the interview was going. "But not if they don't want to hear about it."

"What do you believe about Jesus Christ?" Dr. Kiesewetter asked, leaning back in his chair. "I thought he was a good man who was misunderstood and crucified about 2,000 years ago."

"I believe He is the Son of God, that He came to earth to die for the sins of the world and that after He died on the cross, He rose again from the dead." It came out in a rush, like I was reciting something I'd memorized in Sunday school. Dr. Kiesewetter did not pursue it.

"I see that your parents are missionaries in Vietnam. Do you plan to join them?" He had stumbled onto the one subject I had hoped to avoid. I had no choice but to answer.

"Uh . . . my parents were missionaries in Vietnam, but they're not anymore," I explained weakly, hoping it would be enough. It wasn't.

"Where are they now?"

"They're in heaven."

Dr. Kiesewetter looked up sharply, then softened. "I'm sorry. Did it have something to do with the war?"

"They were killed last year by North Vietnamese soldiers during the Tet Offensive." My answer visibly rocked him.

"I'm very sorry, David. I guess I did read about that in the paper. Do you mind talking about it?"

"I don't mind talking about it," I said, wondering how he'd react.

"How do you feel about it?" Hesitantly, reluctantly, trying not to sound psychopathic, I explained how I had learned to trust God, how I believed that God had a purpose in my parents' death that I did not understand, but that was ultimately good. Dr. Kiesewetter asked many more questions, finally asking me to explain why I believed in the Bible. His questions were not unfriendly, but they exposed me for what I was: a fundamental Christian who actually believed that the Bible was God's inerrant Word; that God still speaks to people and that people who reject Christ or who have never heard of Him will go to a real hell; that Christians have a responsibility to tell the world about Jesus Christ and that Jesus Christ will someday return to earth in the clouds.

Never once did he indicate approval or agreement.

The interview had lasted for nearly an hour and all I wanted to do was escape. Dr. Kiesewetter removed his glasses and leaned back in his chair. A slight smile played at the corners of his mouth and he looked at me directly.

"I haven't been entirely honest with you," he said finally. Although slightly numb, I noticed that there was a different look in his eye. He continued, a smile spreading across his face, "I want you to know, David, that I too am a Christian." He chuckled at the look of surprise and relief on my face.

"David," he continued, "I want to commend you for your courage today. I only wish that when I was in your position many years ago, I had had the courage to speak about my faith in Jesus Christ as openly as you have."

I didn't know how to respond, so I just listened, gripping the arms of my chair.

"I want you in our medical school," he continued, "and I want you to know that I am prepared to do everything in my power to see that you are accepted." In a daze I thanked him, shook his hand and stumbled back to my car. How had it happened, I wondered, that out of the hundreds of doctors on the faculty of the University of Pittsburgh, a Christian doctor had been chosen to interview me?

Several years later, Dr. Kiesewetter told me that the Dean of the medical school had called him up two weeks before the interview. The Dean knew that Dr. Kiesewetter was an outspoken Christian and very active in the Christian Medical Society.

"Bill," he had said, "I have an application here for our medical school and this guy's so hot I thought I'd better send him to you! You'll see when you get the application." The application was mine.

That year there were 2,200 applications for 100 positions in the first-year class at the School of Medicine. While it was true that most candidates applied to several schools, the Dean estimated that there were at least five qualified students for every position available in the United States. Two weeks after the interview, I received notification from the university that I had been accepted to the freshman class starting September 1969. It was a dream come true—accepted at the medical school of my choice—but still no money!

About a week later, Dr. Kiesewetter called me on the telephone and invited me to have dinner with him and his wife the following Friday night. After dinner we would all go to a hockey game. I immediately accepted and wrote down the directions.

When I arrived I was impressed by the large, three-story, beautifully preserved house. I rang the front doorbell. The doctor opened the door and welcomed me in. Never in my life had I been in a house with such plush carpet and lovely furnishings. Dr. Kiesewetter introduced me to his wife and I immediately sensed that I had found a new friend. Since dinner was ready, she led us directly into the dining room.

The sight of the beautifully set table triggered a wave of inner panic. There were two forks, two knives, two goblets and two sets of plates at each place. How was one to know which to use first? Sitting down, I barely averted dipping the end of my tie in the soup!

Mrs. Kiesewetter turned and asked if I would like white wine with my meal. I felt my face turning pink. If I said yes, I would have to drink it and I did not like alcohol. If I refused, they might think I was "holier-than-thou." Mrs. Kiesewetter sensed my predicament. "Are you accustomed to drinking wine with your meals? I know that not everyone is." I gratefully mumbled a negative reply.

By this time, Dr. Kiesewetter had selected a spoon for his soup. Now I knew which one to use. The dinner went smoothly and I began to enjoy myself. After dinner we headed downtown to watch the Pittsburgh Penguins. I had never seen ice hockey and the Kiesewetters had season tickets for seats in the second row on center ice. Although it seemed to me that there was a great deal of violence, I was amazed at the skill of the players and the speed of the game.

After the game we returned to the Kiesewetters' home for ice cream and coffee. Dr. Kiesewetter turned to me.

"David, the reason I asked you to come this evening was so that Mrs. Kiesewetter could meet you." He paused and looked at his wife as if to confirm something. "Now that she's had a chance to get to know you, we would like to invite you to come live with us while you're attending medical school." For a moment I thought I'd misunderstood him, but as I played his words back in my mind, I realized what he had said. These people hardly knew me, yet they were offering to let me live in their home. For a moment I couldn't think of anything to say.

"I think that would be wonderful," I finally blurted. "I'm so surprised I don't know what to say!"

"Of course, we would want you to eat with us when we're home," Mrs. Kiesewetter explained, "and we would expect you to help in the yard and around the house."

"Your staying in the house will help us, too," Dr. Kiesewetter added, as if I needed convincing. "We are often away on trips and this way the house won't be empty." I tried to imagine what it would be like to live in such a beautiful house.

"I'd be happy to take care of the yard work and anything else you might want me to do," I assured them.

And so, in the space of a few hours, the problem of food and lodging was settled. I sang praises to God at the top of my lungs as I headed my Volkswagen bug back to Beaver Falls.

It gradually began to dawn on me that the Lord intended to provide for all of my needs, including the thousands of dollars I would need each semester for tuition and books. Two weeks after that memorable evening, Dr. Kiesewetter phoned again. He knew of a group in Philadelphia called the Pennsylvania Medical Missionary Society. This organization provided conditional grants to medical students planning to become missionaries. If the student served overseas for at least 10 years, the grant became a gift. Dr. Kiesewetter explained that he had called their president and asked her to send me an application. I sent the completed application to Dr. Kiesewetter who added a strong letter of recommendation and forwarded it to the society.

One month later as I read their letter of response, my hands began to tremble: the Pennsylvania Medical Missionary Society was agreeing to pay for my tuition and my books! During the four years that followed, God so wonderfully provided through them and others that in 1973 I graduated from medical school essentially debt-free.

On graduation day as I walked up the steps and was handed my diploma, I wished that my parents could be there to rejoice with me. But even as I wished, I knew that they had already given me everything I needed to follow in their footsteps, especially their example of faith in God.

5

The Mitchells

I have a picture to prove that when I was fourteen months old I was present at the Mitchells' oldest daughter's first birthday. Of course, I don't remember anything about that encounter, but I do remember meeting Archie and Betty Mitchell in 1954 when I arrived at the Dalat School for Missionary Children in Dalat, Vietnam at the tender age of six.

Mrs. Mitchell was my dorm mother. She was firm and fair and at first a little awesome. She seemed to know a great deal about what went on in the hearts and minds of little boys. She was also a great story reader to lonely little boys and she gave a great scrub, even if you were the 15th dirty little kid in the bathtub lineup. Mr. Mitchell, our dorm father, was even more awesome than Mrs. Mitchell because he was very tall and had a scar on his chin.

In later years I learned that he was the only survivor of an explosion from an incendiary balloon

bomb that the Japanese had floated over to the
United States during World War II to set the forests on fire. At that time Mr. Mitchell was a young
pastor in Bly, Oregon. One day, he and his wife
took a group of children on a Sunday school picnic
in the woods. While he was unloading food from
the car the children discovered the unexploded
bomb. Archie shouted a warning, but it was too
late. A tree protected Archie from the blast and he
survived. His wife and all the children were killed
in the explosion. They were the only civilians who
died on the U.S. mainland during World War II as
the result of hostile enemy action.

Mr. Mitchell had big, hard hands that were
very gentle in the bathtub but unforgettable
when applied to one's bottom. From the time I
came to school until I was ten years old, I lived
with the Mitchells in the dorm eight months out
of every year. They provided a stability to dorm
life that I liked. Living with them was very much
like living with a favorite aunt and uncle.

I have already mentioned the Mitchells' oldest
daughter, Rebecca. She was a tomboy. To the
shame of all the boys, she could run faster and farther, jump and climb higher and play softball, bas-
ketball and just about every other game as well or
better than any of us. She seemed to delight in
proving that in every area she was better than the
boys. The fact that her parents were the Mitchells
made the situation particularly difficult. She made
a great point of telling us that if we touched her,
her father would squish any one of us "like a bug."

It seemed totally plausible and naturally this did not endear her to us.

The Mitchells had three other children, all of whom I thought were nicer than Becki.

When I was eleven, the Mitchells returned to the United States. After one year of furlough, they tried to go back to South Vietnam, but the government refused to grant them visas until the following year. When they finally were able to return, the Mission assigned them to work in the city of Banmethuot in the central highlands. Becki enrolled in school as an ordinary missionary kid like the rest of us. She was still very athletic and as competitive as ever, but she no longer tormented us. In ninth grade I finally grew past her and as I matured physically and athletically she no longer posed a threat to my self-esteem. I liked girls to pay attention to me and did my best to impress them. Becki would not be impressed and so I ignored her—until one day when her father was kidnapped by the Viet Cong.

Mr. Mitchell was the director of the Leprosy Hospital about fifteen miles outside of Banmethuot. The staff included one missionary doctor, Dr. Ardel Vietti, and a number of other workers, including Dan Gerber, a young Mennonite agriculturist. The Mitchell children had just arrived home for vacation when the first warnings of trouble came: three bridges leading to the leprosarium were burned by the Viet Cong. They also posted a warning against repairing the bridges. The missionaries, certain that the Viet

Cong were not interested in them personally, continued their work at the leprosarium, fording the streams when they had to drive into Banmethuot.

On the evening of May 31, 1962 the Viet Cong struck again. As Mrs. Mitchell and the children watched in horror, the Viet Cong tied Mr. Mitchell's hands behind his back and marched him into the jungle, along with Dr. Vietti and Dan Gerber. No one ever saw or heard from any of them again.

The news of Mr. Mitchell's kidnapping shocked all of us. After all, if it could happen to Mr. Mitchell, it could happen to anyone's parents.

When the missionary kids returned to school a month later, we watched the Mitchell children with a sense of awe. They did not talk very much about their father. We never saw them crying, although I'm sure they did. Their lives went on as before, except that now they shared a common sorrow that bound them tightly together. I remember wondering how they could stand it day after day not knowing where their father might be or what he might be suffering. But I dared not ask. *What if it had been my father? Would he be locked up in a bamboo cage? Would he be tortured? Marched every day through the jungle? Chained in an underground Viet Cong cave?* The thought of it left me shaken and fearful. *How can they stand it?* It was a great mystery, one that I did not understand until many years later.

In 1965 I left Dalat School for the last time. I don't remember saying goodbye to the Mitchells. It seemed to me that in an indefinable way their experience had left them a cut above the rest of us. After the death of my own parents six years later, in that same city of Banmethuot, I learned that in the school of life, there is no better teacher than godly sorrow.

During my years at Geneva College I kept a sharp eye out for the right girl. I was certain that I would find her during college, since bachelorhood did not appeal to me. Finding the right girl, however, turned out to be more of a challenge than I had imagined. To begin with, I was still trying to figure out the American system of courtship. I was often perplexed. The social structure at Dalat School was designed to discourage kids who lived together from sunup to sundown from getting into serious romances. With such clearly defined goals, circumvention was a relatively simple matter. But my being an artist in manipulating the Dalat social system did not help at all in the United States.

During my senior high school year in America after several humiliating efforts at dating, I decided not to try any more. But teenage hormones being what they are, my interest in girls soon overwhelmed my pride. By the time I graduated from high school I had dated most of the girls in our church's youth group. They probably were of the opinion that I was a nice fellow, but somewhat strange.

In college, however, the business of courtship became a serious matter since marriage was now a

definite possibility. Mother had warned me to be
very careful and had counseled me to ask the Lord
to help me find the right girl. I determined to date
only Christian girls, confident that I would recognize the right one when I saw her. Within a month
I was going steady. The courtship did not last long
and was but the first in a series of short-lived romances bruising to both myself and the girls I
dated. My problem was that if a girl wasn't a possibility for marriage, I wouldn't date her. If I started
dating a girl and she dated someone else, I
dropped her. It was all very intense. Once the girls
found out how serious I was, they wanted to know
a bit more about me. When they found out that I
was planning to become a doctor, the friendship
warmed up. When they found out that I was planning to be a missionary doctor, the relationship either cooled on the spot or gradually unraveled.

   I became somewhat of a loner. After my parents' death, I didn't feel that I belonged to anyone anymore. Yes, I still had my brothers and
sisters, but except for my sister Judy, we were
separated by half a world. Judy and I got together every few months. We realized that if our
family was to remain close we would have to
take the initiative. The problem was that Dale,
Laurel and Tom were still in Southeast Asia,
having been willed to a missionary aunt and uncle, George and Harriet Irwin. The Irwins were
not due to come home on furlough for three
more years. Therefore, Judy and I decided that
we would go to Vietnam. We had an intense

longing to see where Mom and Dad had died and to see their grave.

As usual, we had no money, so we wrote to the Alliance leaders and begged them to help us with the tickets. We knew that sympathetic Christians had donated several thousand dollars to our Alliance Mission headquarters ear-marked for the children of the martyred missionaries. The money was placed in a fund to pay for Dale, Laurel and Tom to go to college. Those who controlled the money did not feel that it was appropriate to use it to pay for our travel. If we wanted to go to Vietnam, they said, we would have to pay our own way.

Their decision was bitterly disappointing. Actually, it took years for me to forgive them. I realize now that those who made the decision thought it was in our best interests, but the effects so splintered our family that it took considerable time and effort to repair the damage. My younger brother assumed that we did not care about him. Twelve long years later, during a belated family reunion, he shared how he had struggled with his anger towards us for our seeming indifference. The wounds are now healed, but I still dream of someday seeing my parents' grave.

But back to my courtship saga at Geneva College.

An attractive girl planning a career in missionary medicine began to show an interest in me. I became so convinced that she was God's choice for me that I didn't bother to ask the Lord. Six months later she explained that I was not the right man for her. My world collapsed. In the pain of the moment, I turned to the Lord for companionship and love. Once again I found that when I hurt the most, God healed the best.

For the first time in my life I began to seriously consider celibacy. Previously the idea had repelled me, but now, still feeling like a boxer the day after losing a big fight, I was ready to think about it. In my heart I hoped I would still find the girl of my dreams, but now I was willing to just do nothing. If there was a right one, God would bring her to me. If there wasn't, I could wait, perhaps forever. Two months later I rediscovered Becki Mitchell!

I was attending summer school and had already been accepted to the University of Pittsburgh School of Medicine for the fall semester of 1969. Because my younger brother Dale was returning to the States from Dalat School, I drove to New York to meet him. At my sister's house in Nyack I learned that one of my former classmates in Malaysia was getting married in a few weeks. We were all invited to a Dalat reunion party at the home of a retired missionary.

As far as parties go, it was pretty tame. The room was crowded and after loading up my plate with cookies and soft drinks I sat down in a corner to talk with some old friends. About half an hour into the evening I noticed a very attractive brunette sitting across the room. I thought, *This is supposed to be a Dalat school reunion, but I don't recognize that girl.* I leaned over to my sister. "Who is that nice-looking girl?" I whispered. When she told me that it was Becki Mitchell, I laughed right out loud. A second look assured me that indeed it was Becki. What a difference five years had made!

She noticed me staring at her. I moved to the other side of the room and introduced myself. To my surprise she was friendly and even remembered me! As we talked, I learned that despite all the years we had gone to Dalat school together, I really did not know her at all. She had opinions, intelligence and a charm that left me feeling warm all over! Forgotten were the days when she outran, outjumped, outclimbed and outplayed me. When it was time to go home I regretfully said goodnight.

"It just doesn't seem fair," I complained to my sister as we got into the car. "The most interesting girl I've met in years goes to school in Tacoma, Washington while I go to school in Pittsburgh!" There was clearly no future in that.

I drove back to Pittsburgh with my brother, a maze of conflicting emotions running rampant through my mind. All week long I prayed about Becki Mitchell, asking the Lord to show me what to do next. By the end of the week I knew what I had to do: pursue her!

The following weekend I decided I should visit my sister again in Nyack. Surely my brother Dale needed to see more of his sister—it seemed only natural! After a nine-hour drive we arrived at 2 a.m. At 8 a.m. the next morning I dialed Becki's number. To my surprise she agreed to go out with me that night.

It was the beginning of a special friendship and a great romance. Both having lost missionary parents, Becki and I understood each other's feelings almost intuitively. We had both struggled, vainly trying to understand God's purpose and both of us had finally ended up holding on to the admonition of Proverbs 3:5: "Trust in the Lord with all your heart and lean not on your own understanding." We had both learned that absolute trust in God does not preclude emotional suffering. Finally, we both had experienced a kind of unconfirmable loss—the ones we had loved were gone, but we had never personally seen the irrefutable evidence of their deaths. My parents and her dad had just sort of disappeared. The only difference was that I knew my parents were in heaven, while she still did not know if her father was dead or alive. As we shared our feelings, the powerful magnetism of common suffering bound us together. It became pure pleasure to drive eight hours—and pay the tolls—every weekend on the Pennsylvania turnpike.

In September we left for opposite ends of the North American continent: Becki to continue her nurses' training in Tacoma and I to begin medical school in Pittsburgh. During Christmas break I had ten days off. A friend of mine wanted to go to California for the break, so we agreed to take his car and share the driving. I was put in charge of the food for the trip and since bologna was cheap, I made forty bologna sandwiches.

As soon as classes were out we started off, changing drivers every two hours. Instead of stopping to eat, we ate the bologna sandwiches I had prepared. At first they tasted pretty good, but by the second day we couldn't stand them. We reached Sacramento, California in forty-eight hours. Becki met me there with her aunt's car and we drove through beautiful snow-covered forests to Klamath Falls, Oregon to spend the holidays with her aunt and uncle.

Within two weeks of that first meeting in Nyack, I knew that I wanted to marry her. I was madly in love with her and I thought she loved me; but would she marry me? It seemed a bit rash to ask so soon. *What if she turns me down? What will I do then?* It was a thought more terrifying than death.

Becki welcomed me so enthusiastically in Sacramento that I took heart. Two days after Christmas and the day before I had to leave, we climbed a hill overlooking Klamath Falls. Snowflakes were drifting down, camouflaging the city lights below in an almost make-believe glow. Alone on the hill, two people embraced. One was enjoying the romantic moment; one was terrified. I was at a crossroads in my life and this girl had the power to crush me or to make me intoxicatingly happy. The only sound in that silent

night was our breathing. I stopped breathing
and asked her to marry me.

I had expected her to stop breathing too, either in shock or astonishment. Surely she would
at least want to think about it for an hour or so.
She might even want to think—no, pray—about
it for a week. When she answered "yes" in the
next breath, I nearly fainted.

"Are you sure?" I asked. "I mean, really?" I
couldn't believe I had heard right. She was laugh-
ing at me. Of course she was sure! She had been
sure of it since the night of the Dalat reunion in
Nyack. That same night she had gone home and
written her mother that she had met the man she
was going to marry. She had been waiting for me
the whole time!

After so many disappointments, I was afraid
to believe that God could be so good to me. As
the months passed and the letters and phone
calls confirmed that her love for me was real, I
began to see more clearly a side of God I had
forgotten—His benevolence. I had seen Him
surround His deeds in clouds of impenetrable
mystery and I had heard Him demand trust and
obedience. Now His goodness, love and kindness unfolded like the petals of a flower in
bloom. He had miraculously provided for all of
my financial needs. He had opened the high and
forbidding gates to medical school and now He
had given me the bright promise that I would
once again belong to someone.

On June 26, 1971 Becki and I were married.

6

Finding the Open Door

Growing up in Southeast Asia seemed to Becki and me to be the perfect preparation for working there. Between the two of us we knew the cities of Saigon, Bangkok, Hong Kong, Phnom Penh, Singapore, Kuala Lumpur and Penang. We were familiar with Asian cultures, thought patterns, religions and geography. So naturally we assumed that we were destined to return to serve God in Asia.

And I was in a hurry. I had a secret fear that Jesus Christ would return before I would be able to do anything important for Him. It wasn't until well into my third year of medical school, after Becki and I were married, that I realized that if the Lord suddenly came He would want to know why I was waiting until I got overseas to start serving Him. So I became active in our local church and helped re-activate the Christian

Medical Society at the University of Pittsburgh Medical School.

By the fourth year in med school I knew what I liked—surgery. But I did not like the idea of five more years of study to become a surgeon. Besides, I wasn't sure it would be all that useful to be so specialized in a Third World country.

I graduated from medical school in May, 1973 and in June began my internship at Mercy Hospital in San Diego.

During the last year in Pennsylvania we applied and were accepted as candidates with The Christian and Missionary Alliance. We would offer to go after my second year of surgical training. Not only was I anxious to get overseas and begin "real missionary work," but I was concerned that if I stayed in the U.S. too long, the attraction of a surgical practice would be too great to resist. I had already encountered many Christian physicians who confessed that at one time they had been planning on a missionary career, but had become so entangled financially, professionally and with family obligations that they had never followed through. I was determined not to join their ranks.

After a pre-appointment interview with the Mission executives, we were appointed for a four-year term to the World Vision Children's Hospital being built in Phnom Penh, Cambodia. Our arrival in July of 1975 would coincide with the opening of the hospital.

A vague feeling of dissatisfaction began to filter through my life. I couldn't put my finger on the problem. Our marriage was happy, I was appreciated by my superiors and colleagues at work and was faithful to the Lord and active in our local Alliance church. In every respect I seemed to be a model Christian.

Those who knew of my parents' martyrdom sometimes treated me as though I had been the martyr. Actually, I had done nothing that other Christians were not doing every day. When my mother-in-law, Betty Mitchell, stayed in San Diego during her furlough, I could see that she knew God in a way that I did not. There was a power in her life that mine lacked. It was a power that put others first—a power to love unlovable people, a power to be meek and at the same time courageous. Her example served to heighten my dissatisfaction.

My hunger to experience God more intimately grew so intense that one Sunday evening, at the close of the service, I went to the front of our small church, knelt at the altar and wept over my spiritual coldness. I knew what I wanted, but how did one become more intimately acquainted with God? I did not even know what to ask the Lord. As I waited there, I heard God speaking to me in my spirit. He was asking me to give Him control not only over my daily life, but also my future. *Could He take my life and do with it as He wished? Could He ask me to do anything, anywhere? In conditions that He would choose? Would I endure hardship? Obscurity? Poverty? Humiliation? Would I serve Him without holding back?*

That evening at the altar, I gave my whole life and future to Him, adding this one condition: *Lord, take my life. Take all of me, only fill this unexplainable void in me with more of You. Please let me have more of your Holy Spirit.* I sensed that a transaction had been made.

As the week wore on, I knew that something had indeed changed. I felt a rekindling of the joy I had felt the day God had healed my broken heart. It was as though spring had returned to my heart. I felt free to talk to my fellow interns and even my patients about Jesus Christ. In that first week I led several of my patients to the Lord. The dissatisfaction I had felt was replaced by a feeling of expectation and an intimacy with God I had never known before. It was an experience that impacted on my work and ministry thereafter. God was doing something exciting in me!

During the latter part of my internship, Becki and I bought a house in a burgeoning suburb of northern San Diego called Mira Mesa. The development included over 1,000 new homes, but not one church within 10 miles. Another family from our church also located there. As we talked together one day, we realized that we felt a common burden to establish a church in Mira Mesa. Our pastor and the district superintendent encouraged us to go ahead. Our involvement in establishing this church was one of the greatest adventures in faith we ever experienced.

In 1974 God blessed us with our first child—a little girl. It seemed that God had overwhelmed the sorrow of our lives with goodness, so we named her Rachael Joy. She has lived up to her name.

As my second year of surgical training neared an end, we began making preparations to leave for Phnom Penh, Cambodia. By early 1975, most of the country was dominated by Pol Pot's Khmer Rouge. Under near-impossible conditions, World Vision completed the construction of the Children's Hospital, flying building supplies into the shell-pocked Phnom Penh airport. The city's future looked doubtful. My surgical chief strongly advised me to remain at Mercy Hospital. In April, the city of Phnom Penh fell to the Khmer Rouge. Not long after, South Vietnam also fell. It was clear we would not be serving as missionaries any time soon in either Cambodia or Vietnam.

Several weeks later the Mission board asked us what we wanted to do. There were three alternatives: medical work in Thailand at a clinic, working on loan to another mission at a hospital in Irian Jaya or medical work in Africa. Africa was simply out of the question, but the opportunity in Irian Jaya sounded challenging.

We set about filling in the application forms for the mission in Irian Jaya where we would serve on loan. The questions and our responses soon revealed that we had some significant doctrinal differences. We could not serve under such circumstances. Once more our plans were frustrated. There was no doubt in our minds that the Lord had clearly called us and had worked many miracles in preparing us for ministry and bringing us together, but now there did not seem to be any place in the world open to us, except maybe Africa. Surely that couldn't be God's will.

7

Slow Boat to Africa

As it turned out, we never did go to Asia because God closed every door. Instead, in September of 1975 we flew to Paris, France, then on to Albertville, where we studied French for a year. Then, for six months, both Becki and I studied Tropical Medicine in Antwerp, Belgium. By March of 1977 we were headed at last for our appointed field—Gabon, West Africa.

Perhaps the best preparation to live and work in Africa is to have to wait a long time. My missionary colleagues will understand what I mean. The longer the wait and the less comprehensible the reason for the wait, the better. Over the previous months of closed doors and altered plans, we had been learning how to wait. However, the major lesson in waiting still lay ahead.

Before leaving Europe we purchased a Land Rover in England. We discovered that if we accompanied the vehicle on a freighter, it could be shipped for half the usual cost. The shipping company assured us that the trip from Marseilles, France to Libreville, Gabon would take about two weeks. What they meant, and what we failed to perceive, was that it would take fourteen sailing days!

We watched our truck being swung up onto the rear deck of the ship in a large rope net. Carolyn Thorson, a nurse also assigned to Gabon, would be accompanying us on the trip. As the ship pulled away from the dock and headed out to sea, we were giddy with excitement.

What a surprise when, two days later, we docked at Genoa, Italy, far to the east of what should have been a direct southerly route. After twenty-four hours of waiting while heavy trucks were loaded onto the ship, we sailed west, this time to Valencia, Spain, where for two more days we waited as workers pumped vast quantities of red wine into tanks in the hold, enveloping the ship in heady fumes. Our enthusiasm for sailing was already beginning to wane. By the time we sailed out of the Mediterranean Sea and into the Atlantic Ocean, a whole week had passed.

As we sailed down the west coast of Africa towards Dakar, Senegal, spectacular weather renewed our spirits. Porpoises frolicked alongside the ship during the day and brilliant sunsets faded into velvety, star-lit skies. Ten days into the trip, we docked in Dakar, Senegal and set foot on the continent of Africa for the first time.

After two days in Dakar, we were on our way again only to drop anchor for two days off the coast of Sierra Leone, waiting to pick up additional crew.

The cargo of wine was unloaded in the Cameroon. Probably not by accident, the crew always managed to overflow the tank trucks. Every time it happened, dock workers rushed madly to the truck to catch the wine running off the fenders, running boards and chassis. To the captain's disgust and to the crew's great amusement, by the end of the second day, half of the dock workers were too drunk to stand and some of the tanker drivers could barely maneuver away from the docks.

It had already been one month since we had embarked on this journey. I had read every book I could find—some of them twice. To help pass the time in the evenings, we made up games with pieces of cardboard. We were thoroughly bored and suffering from cabin fever. Fortunately, our next and last stop was Libreville, Gabon—or so we thought.

We arrived at the Libreville port of Owendo early one evening. The next morning the captain told us that there were so many ships waiting ahead of us to unload that our ship would have to wait for three weeks to get a berth! Aghast at the thought of another three weeks on board ship, we begged the captain to let us off. He assured us that he could arrange it, and so, our waiting finally over, we happily packed up our bags and prepared to leave. The hours dragged on with no sign of the police motor launch that was to take us ashore.

Finally around noon, a boat came out from port and pulled alongside the ship. Several uniformed men climbed aboard and went to the captain's cabin. Soon we heard angry shouting, doors slamming, feet pounding. The two uniformed men hastily climbed back into the launch and to our dismay sped back to port without us. The captain glumly explained that we could not get off the ship—the customs officials had decided to take the afternoon off! We were outraged. How could a country's customs department simply "take the afternoon off?"

"It is the way things are here," he shrugged. "They have put our name on the waiting list and will come back in two weeks." We watched numbly as the ship got underway, heading south to unload and pick up more cargo. Two days later we reached Pointe Noire, Republic of Congo. Since we were Americans, we were not allowed off the ship. The Republic of Congo is a communist state and in 1977 Americans were not welcome.

At Pointe Noire, two Swiss passengers got on board for the return trip to Europe. With obvious relief to be leaving, they recounted a chilling story.

About six months earlier, their twenty-year-old daughter had visited them from Europe. One evening, she and her French boyfriend had gone for a walk in the park that fronts the seashore. An unidentified man suddenly ran up behind them in the dark and struck her on the head with a machete. She fell bleeding and unconscious to the ground. She was rushed to the best hospital in the city where a French doctor examined her and pronounced her wound superficial. He sutured her scalp and sent her home.

The following week she complained of headaches and developed an unexplained fever. Then one day she began having convulsions and one side of her body became paralyzed. Her parents evacuated her by plane to Switzerland where she was diagnosed as having a brain abscess. Had the doctor in Pointe Noire examined her more carefully or had he taken an x-ray, he would have discovered that the machete had penetrated her skull. As a result of the injury and subsequent brain infection, her parents said, she remained partially paralyzed. They did not know if she would ever completely recover. As we listened to the story, we wondered what the future held in store for us in Africa.

At long last the time came to return to Gabon. On May 15, 1977, fifty-two days after boarding ship, we docked at Libreville. Melvin Carter, the field chairman, met and welcomed us.

In the months and years that followed, the Lord had many more lessons to teach us. None, thankfully, took fifty-two days!

8

Bongolo

Libreville, the capital of Gabon, is 540 kilometers to the north of Bongolo, The Christian and Missionary Alliance mission station
which was our ultimate destination. The trip by
road is long and arduous. If the road is in good
condition one can make it in ten to twelve hours.
Prior to the mid '70s, there were four ferries between Libreville and Bongolo with the last one
right at Bongolo. But by 1977 bridges spanned
the rivers at all of these crossings except the
Louetsi River at Bongolo. Bongolo was not
deemed important enough to merit a bridge.

When we finally arrived at the Bongolo crossing, we were astonished to find a primitive,
hand-pulled ferry, just large enough for two cars.
We had been told by our missionary colleagues
that Bongolo was our Mission's pioneer station in
south Gabon, established in 1934 by missionaries
named Fairley and Pierson. How could it be, we
wondered, that after forty-three years of continu-

ous station occupancy, this miserable ferry had not been replaced by a more modern one or perhaps even by a bridge? That we would even ask such a question was an indication of how little we understood Africa!

After crossing the Louetsi River on the ferry, we followed the rutted, dirt road up over the first of a series of hills to a road which ran alongside the river on a high bank nearly fifty feet above the water. A soft, continuous rumbling drew our gaze upriver toward the ninety-foot wide, thirty-foot high Bongolo Falls. To the right of the falls a vertical cliff topped with towering trees rose 100 feet. To the left, on the opposite shore, were some cement and stone channels and a small, square brick building that we subsequently learned housed a hydroelectric plant built by our missionaries in the 1940s. The plant provided the station with twenty-four-hour electricity.

We continued along the high bank for half a kilometer before turning right and up onto a second hill. At the top of this hill we saw a large white church with graceful open gothic windows, a steeply canted roof and a square-topped steeple. It was beautiful despite its need of a paint job. Next to the church was an elementary school consisting of four large buildings and about 100 yards to its left was the dispensary.

I was not mentally or emotionally prepared for the small, primitive building which housed the dispensary. As we entered, about twenty-five curious patients immediately crowded around. Mrs. Sarah Luteijn, a Dutch missionary nurse, beamed with joy and pumped our arms in welcome. One day this dispensary would become the Bongolo Evangelical Hospital, but now, there was only a very inadequate building containing some odd-looking tables and cupboards made out of old shipping crates, a trunk full of medicines and a box of medical odds and ends. Surrounding it were several acres of knee-high grass.

Pastor Ndongo Philippe greeted us warmly. I noticed when I shook his hand that it was hard and calloused. He was very pleased that we had arrived safely but apologized that there were so few people there to welcome us—we were not expected until the next day. We got back in the car and continued up the third hill to the missionary residences.

Here we were struck by the beautiful landscaped lawns, flowering shrubs and giant trees—a real tropical paradise. Combined with the red-brick and white houses, the overall effect was pleasing and inviting.

For the first week we concentrated on settling in and getting used to our new surroundings. Accommodations were inadequate for ourselves and the two new missionary nurses who were part of our medical team, so for the first six months Carolyn Thorson and Joyce Strouth lived in one bedroom while our family occupied the other two bedrooms in the old wooden house called "House Five" on top of the highest hill in Bongolo.

Since most of the people in Gabon speak French to some degree, and because most of the time we would use French in our medical work, we were ready to get to work. The Mission arranged for a veteran missionary to tutor us in a crash course in the Yinzebi language and in the local tribal customs during the first six weeks.

With orientation completed, we were free to give ourselves full-time to the needs of the dispensary and the community. Or so we thought. About that time, the field executive committee met. Soon after, Melvin Carter, the field director, came to Bongolo to see how we were doing.

We were bursting with plans and enthusiasm as we sat down with him in our living room and shared our vision for the development of the Bongolo Evangelical Hospital. He listened patiently and at the first opportunity interjected: "I think you're going to have to put some of your plans on hold for a while." Becki and I and the nurses were stunned by his seriousness.

"Why?" I asked.

"The executive committee has decided that you must first learn the Yinzebi language." His words went off in my head like a bombshell.

"Why?" Becki finally broke the awkward silence.

"We feel that if you are to have a really effective ministry, you must speak the 'language of the heart,' which in Bongolo is Yinzebi." The discussion that followed was tense and dismal.

"I'm sorry that you feel that way," Melvin concluded, "but the decision has been made. I'm
here to tell you that you are to begin studying
Yinzebi thirty hours a week starting tomorrow.
It must take precedence over everything else."

When he left a few minutes later we went to
our separate bedrooms to think. In my heart I
had only one thought: "Just try and make me."

I did nothing about the language study for
several days. However, I was increasingly unhappy so finally decided to make a token effort.
Our progress was impeded not only by my attitude but by the many patients who began coming to the dispensary "because there's a doctor
now." I was inundated with work. The lack of
equipment and adequate facilities made every
emergency difficult and time-consuming. Many
nights were spent working on patients using
only kerosene lanterns for light.

Several months later, our "token effort" mode
still in effect, Becki and I went to visit Julie Fehr, a
missionary to the Mitsogo people at Guevede,
thirty kilometers north and east of Bongolo. We
poured out our complaints to Julie, detailing the
unfairness of the situation. Finally she spoke: "David and Becki, I'm sure you're having a tough time,
but I wonder if you really understand your position as new missionaries. You're here to learn. This
is the best opportunity you will ever have to get
close to the Banzebi people. Maybe you should
accept this decision as from the Lord." I sensed
that God was speaking to us through Julie's words.

"Let me share something from Proverbs that has been of great help to me," she continued. " 'Listen to advice and accept instruction and in the end you will be wise.' And there's one more word I think applies to you. It's something I've found very helpful. 'In the way of acceptance lies peace.' "

Her words flew like an arrow into my heart.

Becki and I hardly spoke as we returned to Bongolo. But after the kids were in bed, we talked far into the night. We realized that in rebelling against the mission leaders we were rebelling against the Lord. He reminded us of His instruction in Hebrews 13:17: "Obey your leaders and submit to their authority. They keep watch over you as men who must give an account. Obey them so that their work will be a joy, not a burden, for that would be of no advantage to you." The Lord also reminded me of the covenant I had made with Him at the altar years before in San Diego—the promise to go wherever and do whatever He told me to do. We asked the Lord to forgive us for our disobedience to our leaders and to Him and purposed in our hearts to do our very best to learn the Yinzebi language.

With the twin pressures of medical emergencies and inadequate facilities, it was still very difficult to concentrate on language study. But because our hearts were willing, God enabled us to complete our studies in only eighteen months. I will always be grateful to Melvin Carter and to the field executive committee for insisting that we take the time to learn the tribal language. It has helped us immeasurably to understand the Gabonese people and to serve them for Christ's sake.

9

The Plan

My introduction to the Bongolo dispensary took place, as I have already mentioned, on the day after our arrival. The dispensary, I learned, had been in operation for almost twenty years. When the Church leaders were informed that the Mission was finally going to send them a doctor, they raised the money and built a fifty-foot by twenty-five-foot mud-brick building next to the dispensary to serve as a ward. When we arrived, the dispensary was treating fifty patients a day, plus the ward was filled with people who were either too sick to come every day for treatment or had no other place to stay.

The dispensary had cement floors which were the same color as the red dirt outside. There were sinks, running water—thanks to the patients—and soap, but the walls needed painting. Patients were consulted four at a time. Nothing was confidential. After a nurse completed the examination and wrote a prescription, the patients moved to an adjacent bench to be served their medicines. Inevitably, at least six people were always talking simultaneously. There were only four light bulbs in the entire dispensary building and none at all in the ward. There were twenty low wooden beds covered with straw-filled cloth mattresses in the ward. There was no ceiling in the room and the walls were not plastered. Orders and treatments were written by the nurse on a tattered notebook that each patient provided.

In addition to the dispensary and ward buildings, there was one outhouse for everyone and one communal kitchen. This building consisted of an eight by ten foot mud-brick house with small, high windows to let out smoke from the open fires. Each patient had to have someone to look after him, cook his meals and wash his laundry. Since the patient's helper usually slept in the same bed as the patient, and since sometimes the whole family came along, the crowding was incredible. I calculated that at least 40 people crowded into that small building at night.

We discovered during our first week in Bongolo that the Mission had a plan for the new medical work and, as is often the case, the Gabonese Church leaders had a different one. At that moment the Mission plan was prevailing in that they were providing the doctor and five nurses. But the Church leaders and members were not happy.

The Mission leaders had concluded that a hospital could never succeed in Bongolo. There was a government hospital four kilometers away in

Lebamba with adequate acute care beds for the district. To build an additional hospital would provide more hospital beds than were needed. If patients wished to be treated in Bongolo, they would have to walk the additional four kilometers from Lebamba and then cross the river. So, the Mission reasoned, with such hindrances there probably would not be enough patients to justify even a small hospital in Bongolo.

An American public health expert, who had previously served as a missionary in Africa, came for a week to look over the situation. He confirmed the board's appraisal and proposed that our medical team live in Lebamba and work in an advisory and teaching capacity at the Lebamba government hospital. The government would provide the buildings and the Mission would provide equipment and supplies with which to establish a vigorous public health program in the area. Once or twice a week the team could go to Bongolo to treat patients at the dispensary. It sounded like a fairly plausible idea.

In Libreville, Melvin Carter took me around to various government offices and ministries for introductions. We were well received at every office, but I was very unsettled by our visit to a high official in the Ministry of Health. The official did not encourage us to work in the Lebamba hospital as we proposed. He would not give us written authorization to do so and suggested that we work it out on a local level. That meant that we, a group of foreigners, would be asking permission of the local director to come into his hospital, equip it, supply it and presumably run it. The plan seemed doomed before it got off the ground.

We were unprepared for both the condition of the Lebamba hospital and our reception there. A Gabonese medical officer—not a doctor—served as the director. He introduced himself to us as Dr. Bayonne. The Gabonese in our party seemed to accept this but I was caught off-balance in that I had been told that there was no doctor in Lebamba. I tried to cover my surprise and shook hands with "Dr." Bayonne.

He took us on a tour of his twenty-four-bed facility. We stepped around animal dung and walked between unpainted and run-down buildings. There was trash everywhere, only partly hidden by high weeds and grass. I saw neither bathrooms nor latrines. There were no showers for the patients and the only water was what the patients hand-carried from a stream fifty yards away. The wards smelled of urine and unwashed bodies and the walls were spotted and smeared. There were no mattresses on any of the beds and the patients lay on their own straw mats or pieces of cardboard that they placed on top of wire springs. There were no charts and the few "nurses" we saw were not in uniform.

Bayonne took us to a private room where he had hospitalized a burn patient. We recoiled at what we saw and smelled. The man was in his twenties and had severe burns over his legs and buttocks. There was not a single bandage on his body. He lay naked on pieces of blood-stained cardboard. As far as I could determine, the only treatment he received was mercurochrome applied daily to the entire burn.

It was clear that a great deal needed to be done to improve the situation, but as I listened to Bayonne, my spirits sank lower and lower. He never once asked for my advice and displayed a condescending and almost contemptuous attitude towards me.

Later that day I asked the mayor of Lebamba who would be in charge of the hospital if we were to help. Somewhat uncomfortably he explained that Dr. Bayonne would be in charge. Any changes I wished to make would have to be with Bayonne's approval.

The following week I visited Bayonne again, this time alone. I asked him what he thought our medical team could do at his hospital. Instead of answering my question, he launched into a one hour explanation of how to treat malaria, obstetrical complications and numerous surgical emergencies. His ideas were bizarre and dangerous. Gradually I realized that this man was telling me that he did not want our help.

Determined not to give up, I again asked how I personally could work with him. He explained that on principle he would have to review all my orders and override any that he might find inappropriate. I am usually a very optimistic person, but by this time it was clear even to me that the Mission plan was not going to work.

I went to the Church leaders to discuss the
Lebamba/Bongolo problem. I had some ideas on
what could be done, but I wanted to hear from
them. They had known all along that unless ordered to cooperate, Bayonne would never agree to
anything that would diminish his own prestige.
They suggested that we place the entire medical
team in Bongolo and enlarge and improve the dispensary into a small, evangelical hospital. How,
they asked, could we ever win people to Christ
while working under Bayonne in Lebamba? They
too recognized the problem of authority. For our
medical team to work in Lebamba would be like
trying to make an elephant fly.

After our discussion, I wrote to the Mission
leaders and asked them to allow us to draw up a
new plan for the medical work after further study
of the needs of the area. They reluctantly agreed.

Six months later, after much study and discussion, the following plan was adopted: (1) the
medical team would stay in Bongolo; (2) we
would develop the dispensary into an evangelical hospital; (3) we would begin a vaccination
program in all of the surrounding villages to control ongoing epidemics of measles, polio and
whooping cough; (4) we would open a nursing
school to train Gabonese nurses for our own
medical ministries in Gabon (the school would
also give us opportunities to develop lay leaders
for the Church); (5) we would open and operate
three satellite dispensaries in outlying villages.

At long last, the Mission, the Church, the Christians, the local government officials, the Ministry of Health and our medical team were all in agreement with what we planned to do in Christ's name in south Gabon. With the acceptance of this plan in 1978, the Bongolo Evangelical Hospital was born.

10

The Outhouse

There was a great deal of work to do at the dispensary to make it into a hospital and even though we had started to study Yinzebi, I felt I had to make some renovations immediately. But what were the priorities?

As a good health officer, I felt I should first insure that there were adequate sanitary facilities. The dispensary's only latrine was a mess, with huge, blue-green flies careening around in dizzying circles whenever anyone entered. The Africans preferred to use the fresh-smelling forest. When, in my best public health officer demeanor, I explained to them that they were spreading diseases and parasites by continuing such practices, they asked me if I myself had ever used the latrine. Since I had not, and since I had no intention of doing so, the discussion came to an unsatisfactory end. One Gabonese characterized the problem most vividly: "When you squat down," he said, with typical African candor, "hundreds of those big flies suddenly fly out of the hole, making a loud, buzzing noise. They bump into you as they fly out." It made me want to run just thinking about it.

Besides the flies, a close inspection of the latrine also revealed an alarming weakness in the central floorboard. If it ever collapsed while someone was using it, well. . . .

I thought about the problem for days. Two of the floorboards would have to be replaced. Since they were the boards with the hole cut into them, I thought it might be a good opportunity to add two more holes. The idea of a three-hole outhouse appealed to my sense of efficiency. Never having used the latrine, the idea that three people might not want to occupy it simultaneously never occurred to me!

I soon became convinced that I should enable our Gabonese people to benefit from western "technology" by teaching them to sit down. I would cut three holes in the boards and would elevate them all the way across the outhouse floor forming a sort of closed-in bench.

Between language lessons, I set to work with enthusiasm. Using our own toilet seat as a model, I traced three holes two feet apart and cut them out. I filed and sanded the edges smooth to make them really comfortable. I then cut out lids and to ensure that they were used, attached the lids with hinges. When the bench was completed, I brought it down to the hospital on the roof of my truck. I assumed that the open mouths of the patients were stares of appreciative wonder.

Norbert, one of the male nurses, helped me unload the thing. He didn't say much as we carried it down the path. It was a struggle to get it into place and nailed down. The clean new wood fairly glowed. I threw DDT into the hole to kill the flies and then showed Norbert how the lids opened up and how the patients were to sit on the seats. I made sure he understood so that he could properly instruct the others. He didn't say much, but seemed to understand. I took one last glance at my handiwork and felt a glow of accomplishment.

About a week later I decided to make an inspection with Norbert. He was reluctant to come with me and I soon understood why. The place was a disaster. I was speechless.

"How is it possible to make such a mess?" I finally asked, trying to control my sense of outrage. Obviously embarrassed, Norbert explained that since the patients were used to the forest, they did not think about keeping the toilets clean.

"How can they miss when they're sitting down?" I persisted.

"Well, doctor," he explained hesitantly, "they don't like to sit down. They say it's unnatural to sit down." Unnatural? I'd done it all my life. How could it be unnatural?

"Well, doctor," he continued, looking away, "it's not that the people don't appreciate what you've done. It's just that the holes are too wide. The children almost fall in." He glanced at me, his tone apologetic. "Also, when they climb up on top of the bench, they hit their heads on the roof," he added. The roof? I looked up. Roofing nails protruded menacingly through the beams of the low ceiling. I winced. So that was the problem. They were climbing up on top of the bench and squatting. The idea that I could teach every Gabonese who used my outhouse to sit down on a seat was absurd. And then it hit me: *Was our western way really better? If so, why?* For the first time I realized that the people would not accept my way just because I was the new doctor. I too had to earn the right to be heard.

The next day the nurse and I grimly removed the bench and replaced it with new boards in the floor and a single hole. It was years before we were able to build all the bathrooms we needed. Now we have all the facilities we need and they are cleaned daily. But since they will never compete with the beauty and privacy of the forest, it continues to be a struggle to get people to use them.

11

Medicine in the Wild

The practice of medicine in the wild can be a rude experience for Western physicians. All initiates expect to have primitive equipment and facilities and to see bizarre and exotic diseases that have been left to mature for years. What Western physicians do not realize is the extent to which their self-image as a physician will be distorted.

Western physicians cherish a position in society second only to God in wisdom, knowledge and skill. Their work may be unique and highly skilled and their time both precious and expensive. They are used to giving orders to myriads of other medical, administrative and technical specialists and seeing them efficiently executed.

In stark contrast, the physician practicing medicine in the wild finds himself alone except perhaps for the help of a few nurses. If he is lucky, some of his nurses will be well-trained. Machines and supplies will be limited or per-

The Thompson family, 1990.
From left to right: Becki (Rebecca), David, Jeremy, Joshua and Rachael.

Louetsi River at the ferry crossing (raft on other side). View from Bongolo side looking toward Lebamba.

Bongolo Falls.

Crossing the Louetsi River. The truck was donated by New Zealand Tear Fund.

The power plant at Bongolo Falls. In 1990 it was destroyed to make way for a new plant that will be built by the Canadian government.

Stuck in the mud. Travel during the rainy season is difficult.

The bridge between Bongolo and Ndende.

A view of the Bongolo Evangelical Hospital, 1989.

The Christian and Missionary Alliance Church at Bongolo.

House #5 where the Thompson family lives.

Patients waiting to see the doctor.

Becki and David with Francois, nurse and lab technician.

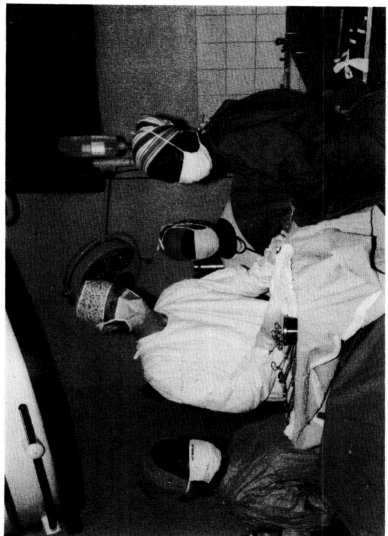

Dr. Thompson and nurses in the operating room.

Students at the nursing school.

The staff at Bongolo Evangelical Hospital.

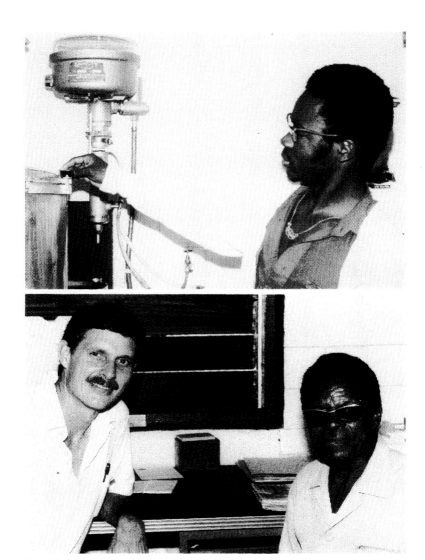

Top: Norbert.
Bottom: David with Mokaya.

haps even nonexistent. Most equipment will have been salvaged from the basement of some North American or European hospital and will not have accompanying instructions.

The western physician coming to Africa either adapts or gives up. Those who adapt learn that medical technology—so wonderful in the west—is sometimes more of a burden than a help. The wise physician learns to rely on his own diagnostic skills and on simple, low-tech solutions to medical problems. He also learns to listen to team members as much as give orders. In simple language, he must lay aside the robes of royalty and put on the blue jeans of humble service.

Having said that, it would be a mistake to conclude that the practice of medicine in the wild is all bad. For the physician who perseveres there will be many interesting and gratifying experiences.

One day I returned early from the Independence Day celebrations in Lebamba. A skeleton crew was running the hospital and on this particular day all of the nurses were women. They told me that a woman nine months pregnant was critically ill and lying on a path "not far" from the hospital. Someone would have to go get her with a stretcher. The girl's mother had walked in and she would show us the way.

I coerced my missionary colleague, Daan Bijl, into helping me and we set off down the path. Thirty minutes later we realized that our perception of "not far" was quite different from that of the girl's mother. We finally found the patient lying on a blanket next to the trail. Both her legs were grotesquely swollen from infection and she was running a high fever.

She had trouble getting onto the stretcher and we had to help her. It was a warm day with about 100 percent humidity. As I struggled with my end of the stretcher, sweat poured off my face and dripped onto hers. She finally covered herself with a towel.

At my insistence, every five minutes or so, we stopped to rest and after fifteen minutes of walking I began to wonder if I was going to make it. Daan was more used to heavy manual labor but I noticed that his shirt was also turning dark with sweat. By the time we stepped out of the jungle and onto the track where we had left the car, my legs were shaking. I had perspired so heavily that my tennis shoes were squishing.

With intensive antibiotic therapy the young woman recovered completely from her infection. One month after arriving she delivered a normal, healthy baby.

A young man named Jean came to our hospital to begin nurses training. As a boy he had contracted polio and his right leg was paralyzed and wasted. He was able to walk, but with each step he had to lock his right knee in extension with his right hand. This required him to walk bent over, leaving him with only his left hand free for work.

Dr. Robert Greene, a missionary orthopedic surgeon, came to visit our hospital and I asked him what he thought about fusing Jean's knee so he could walk upright and have both hands free for work. Bob thought it would be possible but since we didn't have a knee compression device, we would have to manufacture one to squeeze the knee together after the operation so the bone would fuse. Bob came up with a simple low-tech solution. At the conclusion of the operation, he passed a 6-inch stainless-steel nail through the end of the femur bone just above the knee joint and another one through the tibia bone just below the knee joint. The ends of the pins stuck out from the skin about an inch. He then cut an old rubber inner tube into long strips and after bandaging the knee, wrapped the strips around the ends of the nails on each side of the knee joint. The rubber strips pulled the pins toward each other, squeezing the bones together to insure adequate fusion. It was not perfect, but it worked. Today Jean walks with one stiff leg, but upright, leaving both hands free.

Jean's commitment to Christ while he was with us also changed his life drastically. He graduated from the nursing school and got a job working in a remote government dispensary. I saw him about five years later at a seminar we put on to teach primary health care principles to dispensary nurses. Jean told me that he had married, had three children, but had lost them all in one year to malaria. Although he and his wife were heartbroken, they were determined to continue following Christ. I realized then that with our help he had not only learned to walk upright physically, he had also learned to walk and to stand spiritually.

One of my most difficult moments came when I had to operate on my son Jeremy. When he was five years old Becki noticed that he had a congenital hernia. During the following three months it enlarged steadily and since we were not due to return to the United States for three more years, we decided to take care of it in Gabon.

We had two choices: drive 350 kilometers to the Schweitzer Hospital in Lambarene to have it done by a European general surgeon or do it myself. I was operating on Gabonese children and infants almost every week for the same problem, so I felt confident that I could do as good a job on my own child.

We put Jeremy to sleep and in twenty minutes the operation was over. The next day he was up and running around more than he was supposed to. On the fourth day, however, he began to complain of pain in his abdomen. That same evening he ran a low-grade fever. He did not want to eat and by morning the pain had localized to the area of the appendix. The operative incision looked healthy, but I began to wonder uneasily if I had done something wrong. Again we were faced with a choice: treat him ourselves, including possible surgery for acute appendicitis or go to Schweitzer Hospital in Lambarene.

Although it was the week before Christmas, we decided to go to Lambarene because the Schweitzer Hospital's laboratory could perform several tests that might prove helpful. Besides, I was not enthusiastic about operating a second time on my own son.

We left Bongolo around noon. Jeremy was uncomfortable during the six-hour ride over rough, dirt roads, but his condition did not worsen. We arrived in Lambarene around 6:00 p.m. and in a short time a pediatrician came to examine Jeremy. Her husband was the hospital surgeon and he examined him as well. To our relief they both agreed that Jeremy's condition did not warrant surgery that night. As a special courtesy they let us stay in one of their fully furnished staff houses.

The next morning Jeremy was hungry and his blood tests were normal. The two doctors reexamined him and concluded that he did not have appendicitis and was improving. They thought he probably was suffering from a virus. They agreed with me that it was safe for us to return to Bongolo.

We arrived home Christmas eve. It was one of the happiest celebrations our family ever had.

Our missionary/electrician and mechanic went away for a week on a trip and as could be expected a problem arose. I was operating on a patient one morning when a heavy rainstorm swept in and the lights went out. We keep a re-chargeable flashlight for this kind of emergency and one of the nurses held the light while I finished the surgery. I knew it would be up to me to fix the lights. As I was suturing the incision the midwife entered.

"David, I'm afraid I have some bad news. There's a woman in labor and the baby's in trouble. We need you to do an emergency Caesarean section."

I did not want to do such an operation without lights and suction, so I told her to get the woman ready for surgery while I worked on the lights.

I stripped off my operating gown and gloves, ran out the door in my surgical scrub suit and leaped onto my motorbike. By now the rain had stopped, but the ground was wet and water still dripped from the trees. I rode the kilometer to the top of the mission compound where the power lines ended. I needed to see if a tree branch had fallen and either broken the lines or crossed them, causing a short. Starting at the top, I rode under the lines looking for anything abnormal. Two hundred yards down I found the problem: a falling branch had tangled two bare wires together.

Scrounging around in the forest I found another fallen branch long enough to reach the lines overhead. After several tries, I was able to dislodge the branch and untangle the lines.

In the event of a major short circuit, the hydro-electric plant is designed to automatically shut off.

The only problem was that it shuts off on the other side of the river at the generator. To restart the electricity, I would have to cross the river. Grabbing a paddle and balancing it on the handlebars of the motorbike, I raced down the hill to our dugout canoe. It had about two inches of water in it from the rain, but I didn't have time to bail it out. I paddled across the river as fast as I could, drenched with a mixture of sweat, rain and mud. The river was about seventy-five yards wide and by the time the canoe bumped the opposite shore I knew the woman would already be on the operating table. As I paddled, I asked the Lord to protect the baby.

I ran the hundred yards along the forest path to the turbine and generator house, unlocked the door and after assuring that everything was in order, threw the switch back on. The dials indicated that power was back to normal. I ran back to the canoe, re-crossed the river at top speed, leaped back onto the motorbike and raced back to the hospital. The whole procedure had taken twenty minutes.

Panting into the operating room, I quickly washed my hands, covered over my dirty scrub clothes with a sterile, surgical gown and gave the anesthetic. Within minutes the baby was out and appeared to be normal. Despite the demands of medicine in the wild, the Lord had once again helped us to triumph.

12

The Leper's Burial

The old woman paused at the top of the hill to catch her breath and to survey the hospital. She adjusted the woven bamboo strap that supported the small basket on her back. Leaning on her walking stick, she shuffled forward, her swollen, toeless feet sliding slowly over the smooth path. The veins in her neck bulged in the late afternoon sun and several times she wiped her face with a filthy cloth. She had come more than ten miles alone and on foot. Her children had promised to follow in a day or so, but because of her leprosy they had long since ceased to care about her. She knew they would not be coming.

In the waiting area she wearily swung her basket to the ground and rummaged around in it for her notebook. She had only enough strength to carry one cooking pot and a small amount of food in the smoke-stained basket. She finally found the notebook with her medical records, but because some of her fingers were missing she had trouble pick-

ing it up. Finally, she placed it in the basket outside the consultation room window. A few
minutes later a nurse came out, picked up the
notebook and called her into the room.

The nurse examined her and saw that, although she was a leper, she was not dying from
leprosy. She was suffering from advanced con-
gestive heart failure and would have to be hospitalized. Of course she couldn't pay the $2 a day
for hospitalization, but it didn't matter anyway,
since lepers are treated free at the Bongolo
Evangelical Hospital.

I saw her a few hours later. Because there were
not enough mattresses, she was lying on the bare
boards of the bed. She was very dirty and probably
had not washed with soap for years. Her heart was
not only enlarged—it was beating irregularly. She
nodded vaguely when I told her she could eat no
salt. She had several open sores on her feet because the leprosy had deprived them of sensation
and she had injured herself without knowing it.
Her medical record revealed that during the past
five years she had been taking medication for her
leprosy. Although she had lost most sensation in
her hands and feet, the disease itself seemed to be
controlled. I dressed the sores and started her on
treatment for heart failure. I did not notice that
she had no food, assuming that her helper was out
in the kitchen preparing food or visiting with other
patients.

On rounds the next morning I thought she
looked better. The diuretics and heart medicine

were starting to work and she had already lost about two pounds of fluid. I suggested that she ask her helper to wash her clothes and told her that we would supply the soap. She looked down and said nothing. I assumed that she was embarrassed.

The following day she was very weak and it was only then that our nurses discovered that she was not eating because she had no one to prepare her food and could not do it herself. One of the nurses got her some food but she did not want to eat. That night she died.

Early in the morning the nurse on duty called to tell me the news. I asked him to move the body to a private room until we could figure out what to do. I sent a message to a couple of men that had worked for the hospital before, asking them to come dig the grave. Being busy all morning, it was noon before I realized the men had not come. I sent another message asking several men from a nearby village to come. Still nobody came.

The nurses finally helped me place the body into the back of my truck on a stretcher and after loading some digging tools, I drove past the crowd of onlookers and down the hill to the village of Dakar. I started at one end of the village, stopping at the house of one of the church elders and asking him to help. Although he hadn't been doing anything when I arrived, he explained that he was just too busy to help. He recommended someone else for the job, but when I drove to his house and asked him, he suddenly had to help his wife. I

went from house to house, trying to find someone
to dig the grave. Everyone was sympathetic but no
one offered to help.

By about the sixth stop I began to get angry.
Nobody wanted to get involved. I finally roared
out of the village towards the cemetery in a
cloud of angry dust.

The cemetery was covered with low brush and
vines and I had to clear the burial site with a dull
machete before starting to dig. I slashed at the
brush and vines until I had a ten-foot by fifteen-
foot area cleared. I attacked the ground with the
pickax, showering dirt in all directions. My actions, of course, were but a reflection of my
thoughts. I was a doctor and here I was burying
my own patient! Who had ever heard of such a
thing? Sick people would soon expect me to pick
them up at their doorsteps, and after doctoring
them day and night, bury them if they didn't recover. My thoughts were becoming less rational.
By this time I had popped half a dozen blisters on
my soft hands, but I was too angry to even feel
them.

I had already dug the grave to a depth of two
feet when four men from the village walked up,
their faces averted with shame. Without a word
I handed them the tools and stood back to rest.
For the first time I noticed that my hands were
bleeding from the torn blisters.

When the hole was deep enough, we lowered
the body into it and silently filled it in. One of the
men planted a stick at one end of the mound to

mark the grave. I paid the men half the amount I had originally promised, loaded the tools and— still smoldering—left without thanking them.

A feeling of heaviness settled over me. I tried to rationalize it away. *I had buried the woman, hadn't I? I had even dug half of the grave myself. Didn't I have blisters to prove it?* As I tried to justify my attitude, the Lord spoke to me in my spirit. "Why are you angry?" He asked.

"Since when do doctors bury their patients?" I replied hotly. "I should never have had to do that." As I continued up the hill, the Lord asked me another question.

"Why do you think you're too good to bury this woman?" The question caught me by surprise.

"It's not my job to bury people. I'm a doctor, not a gravedigger!" I flashed. As I went into the house, undressed and got into the shower I was becoming increasingly uncomfortable. The Lord finally asked, "David, are you my servant or not?" I stood under the cold water pondering the question.

"You know I'm your servant, Lord," I replied reluctantly.

"Then don't give me this doctor stuff. You are my servant and my servant does whatever I tell him to do." That was all.

As I toweled myself dry, I realized how childishly I had behaved. Being a doctor did not make me any better than anyone else. I began to understand that in God's eyes I was not defined by what I did for a living. Whether I dug graves or repaired hernias changed nothing. I knelt at

the edge of my bed and asked the Lord to forgive me for my anger and for my pride.

When God looks at us, He does not see us as
doctors, lawyers, truck drivers, migrant workers
or whatever else. Although He is very much
aware of the color of our skin, our sex, our intelligence and our level of education, He does not
define us by those things. He only sees us as
willing or unwilling, proud or humble, useless or
useful, disobedient or obedient servants.

13

Safari

We had been in Gabon only about three months when I was asked to take the Webbs, a newly arrived missionary family, to their assigned post in southeastern Gabon. Returning missionaries Enid Miller and Ray and Maurine Holcomb would complete the caravan. The Mission's old, four-wheel-drive five-ton Dodge truck would carry the barrels, crates and trunks; my new Land Rover and the Holcombs' car would carry the passengers.

We left Bongolo at 7:00 a.m. and snaked slowly east and north over the infamous National Highway Number Four from Lebamba to Mimongo, to Koula Moutou and finally to Moanda. The dirt road was poorly maintained and extremely rough. In places the rains had eroded two and three-foot ditches that the cars had to straddle. In other places the log bridges were rotting and partially destroyed. In the rainy season it would be nearly impossible to make the trip, but since it was the dry season, we did not have to plow through four-foot deep mud holes.

We arrived in the town of Koula Moutou after twelve hours of hard driving, averaging only ten miles per hour. The mission house had been closed for a year and the furniture and floors were covered with dust. We were too tired to care and after a dinner prepared from cans, we fell into bed.

Enid Miller and the Webb family would be staying here in Koula Moutou. In the morning we unloaded their things from my car and from the truck. Enid's car had been stored in Moanda during her year of furlough, so she accompanied us as we continued on. Wayne Webb came along too to help unload the heavy barrels and crates at our destination.

I left my car in Koula Moutou and rode in the cab of the truck with Ron Israel, a veteran missionary who had served for years in Guinea before coming to Gabon. He maneuvered the big Dodge over the twisting, rutted roads with apparent ease. We arrived in Moanda around 2:00 p.m.

Moanda is Gabon's manganese mining center and although it is far into the interior, it is more developed than the area around Bongolo. The mission houses here had not been lived in for a year either and, surrounded on all sides by knee-high grass, had a distinctly wild look about them. By 4:00 p.m. we had unloaded the truck and moved the Holcombs' drums and crates into their attic.

Ron and Wayne decided to return immediately
to Koula Moutou, preferring to travel in the cool
of the night. Mrs. Holcomb dusted off the stove,
dug out some dishes, pots and pans and created
an appetizing meal for the rest of us. Many
Gabonese friends came by that evening to welcome Enid and the Holcombs back to Moanda.
We were visiting with some of them when about
8:00 p.m. Wayne opened the front door and
walked in. His sudden appearance startled us. He
and Ron had left four hours earlier—it could only
mean that something had gone wrong.

Wayne confirmed our fears. A front wheel bearing had burned out. Ron had parked the truck on
the side of the road surrounded by dense jungle. A
replacement bearing would have to be found. He
had stayed with the truck to protect it from thieves
and Wayne had hitched a ride with a passing vehicle. The question, of course, was where in the middle of Africa were we going to find a front wheel
bearing for a seven-year-old American truck? To
our knowledge and true to missionary tradition, it
was the only truck of its kind in the entire country
that was still running. We bowed and prayed, asking God to help us find a solution to our dilemma.
Ray Holcomb suddenly thought of something.

"Wait a minute, wait a minute!" he almost
shouted. "The Peace Corps used to have some
of these same trucks up here."

The Peace Corps had had a relatively large aid
project going in the Moanda area seven or eight
years back which included ten or fifteen volun-

teers and three or four Dodge trucks. A sudden
shift in the political climate, a careless word or
deed, and the government angrily ordered them
out of the country. Nobody could remember ex-
actly why anymore. In leaving, they did something
to the trucks to render them useless. After a few
years, their camp was overgrown by ten-foot high
grass. It had been built behind a village near
Moanda and every dry season the people set fire
to the tall grass. What remained of the camp
burned to the ground. The trucks also burned,
year after year, until there was nothing but their
rusted, blackened carcasses, hidden in the dense
brush and high grass. The village was only a few kilometers out of town and Ray was sure it would be
simple to locate the old camp behind it. If he and I
could find one of the trucks and could get a bearing off of it, we could take Ron the part in the
morning on our way back to Koula Moutou. It
seemed pretty far-fetched to me, but I was new
and not in a position to offer advice.

Ray found one good flashlight and a Coleman
lantern, loaded his tools into the back of his car
and we set off on the wildest search I've ever
been on. He drove straight to the village on the
outskirts of Moanda.

A small fire burned in front of one of the houses
near the road. Ray and I stepped into the firelight
and saw several children and an old man. He acknowledged us suspiciously. Ray tried to explain
our mission, but the old man only smoked his pipe
and refused to look at us. Ray persisted, asking the

man to help us find the trucks in the brush behind
the village. At last he responded.

"Tonight?"

"We need to find the truck tonight so we can
take the part to Pastor Israel tomorrow morning," Ray explained.

"Not tonight," was all he said. There was no
point in arguing. The other houses in the village
were already closed up for the night.

"We'll have to find it ourselves," Ray decided.
"I'm sure we can do it. Let's get the lantern." We
went back to his car and lit the Coleman lantern.
The old man turned his head as we walked past
him and through the village, but he stayed in his
chair. I was prepared to work all night taking apart
some old pile of junk, but as we followed a path
into thick, tall brush I began to feel uneasy. Wasn't
this country famous for its venomous snakes? I
had seen a Gabon viper in the San Diego zoo
years before and even behind two panes of glass it
was fearsome. Now I was crashing around in its
territory. And what about cobras? It looked like a
perfect place for cobras. Ray didn't seem bothered
by the thought of hostile creatures, however, so I
meekly followed him around vegetable gardens,
over crude stick fences and along barely visible
paths that he somehow saw in the light of the
Coleman. When he thought we were close to the
camp he abandoned the path altogether, heading
directly into the ten-foot high grass. In the stillness
of the night we sounded like elephants. In my
mind I visualized my epitaph: Dr. David Thomp-

son: 1948-1977. Trampled by enraged buffalo—
after being bitten by a Gabon viper.

After ten minutes of crashing around we
bumped into a high tension line pylon. To be on
a life-threatening safari in the African brush and
run into an electric pylon was culture shock in
the extreme. Despite the incongruity, it represented safety, and when Ray suggested that we
climb the pylon to see if we could see something
from high up, I was only too happy to clamber
out of the reach of the vipers.

We climbed up about thirty feet, only vaguely
conscious of the wires passing overhead. Ray then
leaned out, holding the Coleman up over our
heads as we peered into the brush below. The lantern was so bright we could see nothing. Discouraged, we climbed back down and contemplated
our next move. Ray thought we should strike out
in one more direction.

A new sound! At first it was distant and we
paid no attention, but within minutes we realized it was coming toward us from several directions at once. Seconds later we recognized angry
human voices. It did not take any cultural in-
sight to understand that we were in serious trouble. A minute later about ten men surrounded
us, shouting and slashing the brush in fury. They
were frightened, but more angry than frightened. As sweat poured off their faces and their
heaving chests, they screamed incoherently at
us. It must have been difficult for them to comprehend what they were seeing. Why would two

strange white men be wandering around in the brush behind their village at 10 o'clock at night?

As the junior missionary I thought it best to allow Ray to save us. The angel of the Lord must have given him courage, because while my mouth was frozen open, he began speaking in Yinzebi. This was the language of our captors and it both surprised and calmed them. As Ray explained our mission, the men gradually lowered their machetes to more reassuring angles. Little by little, he convinced them that we were really missionaries and that we were interested in the old Peace Corps trucks.

After about ten minutes of talking and explaining, Ray was able to enlist their help. He offered to pay them something and all hostility evaporated. The men fanned out in ten different directions. Within minutes we found one of the trucks. Ray ran back to the car to get his tools while I cleared away some of the brush.

The tires had long since burned away but it was not difficult to get a jack under the front axle and lift the wheel up off the ground. The bolts were rusted solid, but by using a steel chisel we were able to loosen them and eventually pull the wheel off. Thirty minutes later, we reverently lifted out an almost-perfect front wheel bearing, still slippery with grease. It was too much to believe that it would fit our Dodge. Ray paid each man about $2 and we returned home giddy with relief.

The following day I helped Enid Miller get her car out of storage. The car started easily and we drove back to the mission to get ready to leave for Koula Moutou. A local Gabonese elementary school teacher had asked us the night before if he and his wife could accompany us to Koula Moutou. Since I was going to drive, Enid wanted me to decide about the passengers. I agreed to take two passengers and two suitcases, enough to comfortably fill the small Land Rover.

The next morning I suggested that the teacher put his two suitcases in the car while Enid and I ate a bit of breakfast. When we came out of the house to leave, I was surprised to find a crowd of about 10 people standing around the back of the car. The teacher was not in the car, but his wife and three other people were. And there were at least six suitcases and sacks of food crammed inside. The teacher seemed hurt when I ordered everybody out of the car. One person finally climbed out, but nobody touched the bags.

The others looked at me as though my French had suddenly become too heavily accented to understand. I felt my neck begin to redden and a hot flash went through me. It took every bit of my rapidly collapsing self-control to keep from screaming at the remaining two passengers. More calmly than I felt, I pulled some of the baskets, suitcases and sacks of food out of the car. One more passenger climbed out. With Enid already in the car, I closed the back door and drove off, my emotions raging.

"That's why I wanted you to handle the problem," Enid finally said. "It happens every time. Get used to it."

"What would you have done?" I asked when I felt calmer, knowing that I had concealed my anger poorly. She sighed and shook her head.

"I'd have made them all get out, but you did fine. They were testing you. Now they know what to expect of you."

"What if I had given in?" I wondered aloud.

"Then you would have to get used to people ignoring what you say," she explained with a laugh.

"What if people simply refuse to get out of the car?" I asked.

"Oh, I've learned a few tricks," she chuckled, "but they require more patience than you have at this point!" What were the tricks, I wanted to know.

"I just remove the keys, get out of the car and announce that the car will not move until they get out. Then I go find a comfortable spot to sit down and rest. Eventually, those who aren't supposed to be there get out and I am able to continue on." I had to laugh at the simplicity of the idea. Two hours later we pulled up behind the broken-down Dodge.

Ron could hardly believe that we had found another bearing. It took less than an hour to replace the old one. Ron drove ahead of us the rest of the way to Koula Moutou. That afternoon we said goodbye to Enid and the Webbs and headed back down the road to Bongolo.

It was extremely hot and driving my car mile after dusty mile behind the Dodge made me very thirsty. By nightfall we had drunk all of our drinking water. We stopped for the night in a village where there was a church and were warmly welcomed by the head elder. His wife served us a delicious meal, but we were so thirsty we could hardly taste the food. They offered us water, but knowing it was unsafe to drink, we politely declined. Neither of us had the courage to ask them to boil water for us to drink, so we went to bed with dry throats.

In the morning our hosts boiled water for coffee and seemed surprised that we drank so many cups. By 7 we were back on the road and drove with thirst-driven intensity dreaming of the ice-water we would drink on arrival at home. We pulled into Bongolo around 3 p.m. covered so evenly with red dust that only our eyeballs looked clean. Cold water never tasted so delicious.

I have often marveled at the way God provides for his people, but this experience stands out to me as one of the most amazing. In the middle of the African rain forest, God perfectly preserved a front-wheel bearing for a seven-year-old American missionary truck. Surely it is for these kinds of experiences that the Apostle Paul wrote, "And my God will meet all your needs according to his glorious riches in Christ Jesus" (Philippians 4:19). Not only does our God own the cattle on a thousands hills; He owns all the wrecks, too!

14

The Goat War

S oon after my experience with the outhouse, I took on the goats. The goats were one of the first things we noticed when we arrived in Bongolo. They were everywhere—running freely over the Mission property, the dispensary grounds, even standing defiantly in the open church windows.

About 100 goats considered the dispensary to be their home and everywhere they went they left traces of having been there. The droppings were especially dense on the steps in front of every doorway and on the paths from those doors. Inevitably, the floors of the dispensary were tracked and dirty. By the end of each day the droppings were dry and were swept out of the dispensary in clouds of dust. Eventually goat dust coated everything. A better scenario for introducing tetanus into open wounds could not be devised. It was my solemn duty and obligation to rid the dispensary of this plague.

During our first few weeks, I observed the goats carefully. Although they were surrounded by acres and acres of fresh grass and succulent vegetation, they continually wandered through the dispensary courtyard, rubbing themselves along the walls. Every building in Bongolo had a brownish six-inch wide line running around its base. In open surrender, the dispensary committee had ceased to paint the lower four feet of the outside walls of the building.

It was clear that something had to be done. I started by asking my staff to throw stones at the goats whenever they saw them around the buildings. They were less than enthusiastic and by the end of the first week I was the only one carrying on the fight. For months, whenever a goat came within range, I interrupted whatever I was doing to stone it. The goats soon learned to scatter when I appeared to be looking for a stone. In order to inflict pain, I had to be more subtle. Whenever I saw a goat, I would casually glance around until I spotted a stone. Feigning complete indifference to the goat, I would saunter over to the stone, then in a blur of motion, I would pick up the stone, pivot and hurl. This technique reduced my accuracy to almost zero. Not appreciating the seriousness of the problem, the Gabonese—and even my staff—thought the routine was quite comical.

After six months of battle, the goat deposits remained as abundant as ever. The goats were simply staying out of range when I was there and returning with a vengeance at night. Unwilling

to accept defeat, I resorted to modern technology: I bought an air-powered pellet rifle.

Conditioning was the key to the problem I decided. I had to somehow condition the goats so
that they would associate the hospital grounds
with stinging pain. In order to succeed, I reasoned, I would have to consistently apply the
conditioning.

It occurred to me that an occasional goat
might die, but by this time, nothing would have
cheered me more than the sight of goat carcasses all over the hospital lawns. That would, of
course, create major palavers! The goats represented wealth and every goat belonged to someone. How the Gabonese kept them straight I'll
never know, but they knew which goat belonged
to whom. Before escalating to the air-gun,
therefore, I consulted our local pastor.

Pastor Philippe advised patience, but I sus-
pected that he was thinking more about saving
his goats than helping me with the problem.
However, when he realized that I was serious,
he agreed to announce in church the following
Sunday that if people did not remove their goats
from the hospital plateau within one week, the
doctor would begin shooting them!

The next Sunday morning he made the an-
nouncement. After a moment of shocked silence, a murmur of disapproval filled the air.
Every eye turned to see my stern face. When the
pastor rang his little brass hand bell for order the
service resumed.

The goat-owners had one week to corral their
animals. A few of the more sincere ones actually
came and caught some of their goats. This required two highly athletic individuals and several
lengths of expensive rope. Shortly, however, the
goats chewed through the ropes and returned to
the hospital. The net effect was zero. I waited with
growing relish for the week of grace to end.

Monday morning dawned bright and clear. It
was a perfect day for hunting! I made my rounds
at the hospital and consulted patients all morning.
In the afternoon I returned to the hospital with
the air rifle and a pocket full of pellets. The ensu-
ing hunt was emotionally cathartic. The months of
helplessness were forgotten in the glory of seeing
bawling goats run into each other trying to get
away from the sting of the pellets. I hadn't realized
how stupid they could be. It took each goat about
five hits before it associated the pain with the pale
man standing nearby pumping the stick! It took
another two or three hits before the goat figured
out that it could escape the pain if it left the area at
high speed. Within twenty minutes there wasn't a
goat in sight except for three carcasses lying on
the ground. Unfortunately, the three dead goats
belonged to Pastor Philippe!

Much to his credit and to my relief, Pastor
Philippe accepted the loss of his goats as the
price for having a doctor and a hospital. But although the battle was won, the war was not. The
goats returned the next day and had to be recon-
ditioned. By the end of two weeks, only a few of

the more stubborn ones remained around the hospital. They had somehow figured out the range of my weapon and as soon as they heard me pumping the gun they would scurry away.

The goat war considerably disrupted my hospital routine. I took to carrying the gun with me on rounds, already pumped up. If I saw a goat in range, I stopped whatever I was doing to get it in my sights, sometimes even shooting out of the windows of the wards. The children at the hospital joined in the game, running up breathlessly to tell me that a goat was hiding on the other side of the building.

By the end of a year (yes, that's right—a year) of battle, I began to smell victory—literally. There remained, however, a few clever goats that would not concede defeat. They stayed away during the day but returned at night when they knew I was not around. In the morning when I came down to work, the sight of droppings all over the benches in the waiting area and courtyard made my blood boil.

By this time I knew what the offending goats looked like and one afternoon I decided to go after them. I found them browsing in the forest on the other side of the church. They heard me coming and scuttled into the thick underbrush. Although I was wearing my hospital whites, I decided to go in after them. Carefully working my way through the thick brush, I circled around behind them, making a great deal of noise to scare them out into the open where I could get a clear shot at them. They wisely chose to stay hidden.

I moved closer, stepping up onto a fallen tree. Just twenty feet away I saw an inviting, furred rump. I brought the gun to my shoulder, sighted down the barrel onto the brown fur and began to squeeze the trigger. Suddenly my legs felt like they were on fire. In my excitement to shoot the goats, I had stepped onto a column of army ants. Army ants have a wonderful ability to incite frantic and bizarre motion in large animals and humans. At that moment, the only thing in the world that mattered to me was to get off that log, get my pants off and get rid of the ants that were burying their jaws into my flesh. Thrashing and leaping about in the underbrush, I finally managed to do just that. It took about two minutes to tear the big ants off and another five minutes to find all the little ones. I was relieved to see that no humans had witnessed the antics.

I got my pants back on and stepped out of the forest. Both my dignity and resolve were now back in place. I was not ready to admit defeat. As I came around the corner of the church building, I saw the receding rump of a white goat. I threw the gun to my shoulder and fired. To my surprise, the goat dropped in its tracks. I walked up to it just in time to see it take its last breath. With amazing accuracy the pellet had entered the goat's skull from behind in an unprotected spot.

Two days later, Pastor Philippe dropped by the house for a visit. We exchanged news and chatted for a few minutes before he fell silent, began to rub his hands and clear his throat. Obviously he had something he wanted to say. "Do you remember the goat you killed the other day, doctor?" he asked finally. I told him that I remembered. He cleared his throat again. "It was Lebongo Antoine's animal." I didn't know Lebongo Antoine very well, except that he was a schoolteacher in the local elementary school. He was known for his heavy drinking and his bad temper and whenever he came to the hospital he was rude unless he received preferential treatment. He had always been respectful to me, however. The pastor continued. "Lebongo was very angry that you killed his animal. Last night he drank too much and told his drinking buddies that he is going to get revenge." I was not afraid of Lebongo Antoine. What could he do to me?

"He told them he was going to do something to your children." A chill crept into my heart. Our daughter Rachael was five and Joshua was two.

"How serious is he?" I finally asked.

"We don't know," the pastor answered, "but the whole village knows about this threat and everyone is angry with him. He won't do anything openly, but he's a difficult man and at the very least he will put a curse on your children." Assuming that as a Christian I was automatically protected from evil spirits and understanding very little about spiritual warfare, I was not too concerned.

"What do you suggest I do?" I asked. "Should I go and apologize?" The pastor didn't think I should apologize. After all, hadn't I shot everybody's goats? Hadn't I warned everybody first? "Perhaps," he suggested, "you could just frighten away the goats for a week or so until things quiet down. In the meantime, you will have to trust God for the safety of your children." We prayed together and the pastor left. After he had gone, Becki and I got on our knees and recommitted ourselves and our children to God, placing us all under His protection.

I did not see Lebongo Antoine again before returning to the United States because shortly after that incident the church leaders used their influence to send him to teach in another town eighty kilometers away. It was not, however, the last I would see of him.

And what about the goats? They are still a problem. Every goat born in Bongolo seems to have to learn the hard way that to linger at the hospital is to sometimes experience inexplicable discomfort. The goats have not wearied of reproducing, but I have wearied of the battle. Perhaps the time has come for newer technology. A laser goat-vaporizer would suit me just fine!

15

Norbert

When we first arrived in Bongolo, Mouelet Norbert was the only Gabonese nurse working at the dispensary. It was through Norbert that I began to be aware of the struggles the African Christians experience and to admire their faith.

One day Norbert came to work with a very long face. Since he was usually a cheerful person, we noticed the change immediately. I asked him what was bothering him and the story he told was so strange I found it hard to believe.

"I may lose my wife," he said. "Please pray for me."

"What's going to happen to your wife?" I asked, trying to hide my surprise. With eight children, I thought it strange that he might "lose his wife."

"Well," he sighed, "my wife's uncle has promised to break up our marriage and force her to return to her parents with all of the children." He was nearly in tears. Obviously, it was a very strong possibility.

"Why would your wife's uncle want to break up your marriage?" I asked.

"Revenge," he replied.

"Against you?"

"No, against my uncle who lives in the same village." I found this hard to understand, but since he didn't seem to mind my prying, I persisted.

"Why does your wife's uncle want revenge against your uncle?"

"Well, it's a long story." He began to recount what had happened. When Norbert and his wife cleared a piece of land for a garden years before near their village of Idembe, they planted some palm trees in the half-acre plot. The trees produced palm nuts and over the years the palm nuts that fell produced many more trees. After Norbert and his family moved to Bongolo, both uncles declared the plantation to be theirs and both regularly tapped the palm trees to make palm wine.

It was risky work for old men, because they had to climb to the top of tree, push a thin, hollow tube into the heart of the trunk and leave a bottle to collect the sap. The next day they reclimbed the tree, collected the bottle and climbed down without spilling or dropping it. Each of them wore a belt made out of vines or bark that could be passed around their waist and around the tree trunk. Leaning back against the belt, they were able to walk up the trunk. Every few feet they would stop, quickly lean forward to take their weight off the belt, and using both hands, flip the belt higher up on the trunk. If their feet slipped or the belt broke, the result could be fatal.

One day Norbert's wife's uncle went to the plantation to collect a bottle he had placed in a tree the day before. Arriving at his tree, he found Norbert's uncle emptying the full bottle into his own. Enraged, Norbert's wife's uncle climbed the tree to settle accounts. Norbert's uncle finally knocked his opponent out of the tree. When he hit the ground, he broke his leg.

Both men were lucky to be alive, but the fight was far from over. The local witch doctor splinted the broken leg and, because it was a simple fracture, the uncle eventually recovered. The family, however, plotted its revenge.

Norbert was the only wage-earner in the entire family. His meager income supported his wife, eight children and to some extent both uncles and their families. He was still paying his wife's family her dowry, since among the Banzebi people the dowry is paid until the in-laws are completely satisfied. That can sometimes take a decade. So Norbert was not only providing income for his own parents and uncles, he was also providing income for his wife's side of the family. Nevertheless, his wife's family decided that revenge was more important than income.

The best way to get revenge, they decided, was to hurt the other family and the best way to do that was to break up Norbert's marriage. Since in Banzebi culture a couple's children belong to the wife and her family, they decided to insist that Norbert's wife return home. She would, of course, come with all of the children. If Norbert wanted them back, he would have to negotiate for them and his in-laws would demand a high price as a means of getting even for the broken leg. It was a kind of jungle litigation.

By the time Norbert explained all this, I was as depressed as he.

"But why can't your wife just refuse?" I wondered aloud. "Doesn't she love you?" He pondered the question for several minutes.

"Well, I don't know," he finally answered. I asked him what problems he and his wife were experiencing.

"We haven't been having any problems, except between our uncles," he replied. Yet he didn't know if his wife loved him! My western worldview was finding it difficult to comprehend such a structure. As I persisted in my prying, he explained that Gabonese husbands and wives rarely if ever express their love for one another but that does not mean that they are not devoted to each other. Norbert did not want his wife to leave him, but neither did he want his wife to be a pariah in her own family. If she opposed her family in this matter, her family would renounce and shame her. Rather than face down his wife's family and insist that she stay with him, he felt he should try to negotiate. I could see the wisdom of his tactics, but I was disturbed that his Christian wife would even consider leaving him in order to please her parents.

Norbert asked to have the next day off from work so he could go talk with his in-laws. I gave him permission, promising that all of us would pray for him. The next day, as we worked, we prayed for Norbert. Norbert had not returned by late afternoon. We would have to wait to find out what happened.

The next day Norbert was smiling.

"What happened?" I wondered aloud.

"Well," he said, "when I got to the village, nobody was expecting me. I asked both families for a meeting to settle the problem with the village chiefs present. At first I was afraid they would refuse, but the Lord was with me and they finally agreed to discuss the matter in the afternoon." Several nurses gathered around to listen as he continued.

"We met in the palaver house in the center of the village. One family sat on one side and the other sat opposite. The village chiefs sat at the end to 'hear the matter.' I spoke first, explaining once again what had happened. Then I told them that my wife and I had had nothing to do with the fight, so why should we be punished? The Lord helped me to present my case well and the elders were sympathetic.

"The two sides argued back and forth for hours. Finally, the elders made their decision. I would have to pay my wife's uncle 20,000 francs (about a month's salary) to settle the problem. His family was not satisfied, but because the Lord was with me, the rest of the village made them accept the decision. Isn't that a wonderful answer to prayer?"

I failed to see how it was such a wonderful answer to prayer, but obviously he felt he had gotten off very lightly. Although it seemed to me that a month's salary for something your uncle did was a stiff penalty, I rejoiced with him that his family had not been broken up. It was perhaps a measure of his love that a month's salary was a small price to pay to keep his family intact. I was amazed that he held no bitterness in his heart against his in-laws.

The more I learned about Norbert the more I came to respect him. He represented the second generation of Christians in south Gabon. His parents had sent him to school in Bongolo, since at that time there were no other schools. The Bongolo school, established and operated by North American Alliance missionaries, was taught in the Yinzebi language rather than French. The schools that the government subsequently established in Lebamba and throughout Gabon were taught in French. So, in 1948, when Norbert graduated from sixth grade, he read well in Yinzebi, but could neither speak nor read French. This made it impossible for him to transfer to the government high school to continue his education. The only option for further education was the Alliance Bible school, but he did not want to become a pastor or an evangelist.

Instead, he got a job in Lebamba as a storekeeper. In the evenings he studied French with some of his friends. He worked in the store for eight years, learning French on his own. He picked a wife from his home village of Idembe, saving most of his earnings to pay the dowry. During the eight years that Norbert worked for him, his employer never once lost any money. Although the storekeeper praised Norbert for his unusual honesty, when he decided to move his store, he did not take Norbert with him. Norbert was out of a job.

Hearing that there were job opportunities up north in logging, Norbert took his wife and two children to the logging center of Ikouk, 250 miles to the north of Bongolo. He got a job cutting and planting okoume trees. The okoume tree is valued highly in Gabon for its beautiful wood grain, its resistance to moisture and its workability. It is used to make plywood for export to Europe.

Cutting trees in the central African rain forest is dangerous work. The green mamba, one of the deadliest snakes in the world, lives in the trees. The Gabon viper and the rhinoceros viper, both feared for their deadly bite, live in the dense underbrush. During his years at Ikouk, Norbert had many close calls with poisonous snakes, but never once was bitten. Again and again, the Lord protected him.

Norbert's unusual honesty and hard work caught the attention of the French foreman and he was promoted to greater responsibility. In spite of the good wages, Norbert was not happy at Ikouk for he was the only Christian in the entire camp. Every Sunday he and his family held a service in their home, but Norbert had little training in the Word of God. He realized that his family was becoming increasingly like the pagans around them.

In 1972, Norbert made a life-changing decision: it was more important to honor God than to keep his job. He decided to move back to Bongolo where his family would learn the Word of God. Even at the age of thirty-five, he would trust God to provide him with another job and another career.

Soon after, Norbert visited Irene Shank, the missionary nurse in charge of the dispensary at Bongolo. In addition to treating patients, she trained one or two nurses every year. Irene agreed to train Norbert as long as he understood that she was not obliged to hire him when he finished his training.

Norbert graduated in 1974, but as there was no money to hire him, he offered to work gratis at the dispensary. For two years he worked full-time without pay. His wife farmed to support the family. Norbert's maturity, faithfulness and gentleness with the patients eventually paid off. When we arrived in 1977, he was the only African nurse employed by the dispensary.

Today, Mouelet Norbert is the best nurse we have. He is not the brightest, nor the quickest, but even though he is in his late 40s he remains teachable and enjoys learning new things. Since 1977 we have trained nearly 100 nurses. Norbert has been a model of a truly caring, Christian nurse. There is no job too dirty or too demeaning for Norbert. His gentleness has earned him the respect of the entire community.

Norbert is also one of the most faithful Christians I know. Not only does he care about his patients' physical needs, he also talks with them about their need for salvation in Jesus Christ. It will be a great day in heaven when the many people Norbert has tenderly cared for and led to Christ come to thank him.

16

The Man with Two Wives

We had been in Bongolo for about a year when a man with a bowel obstruction walked in from a village seven kilometers away. His abdomen was quite distended and he staggered slightly as he came up the last hill to the hospital. The nurses laid him down and called me.

Sam Zylstra, an American medical student on a Third World Medicine elective, was already surveying the man's bloated abdomen when I arrived. We started an IV to rehydrate him, and began to discuss what we were going to do.

At the time we didn't yet have an operating room or operating instruments. He also needed a suction tube passed through his nose into his stomach to try to decompress his abdomen. Unfortunately we didn't have the right tubes. The decision was finally made to take him to the nearest hospital that had a surgeon.

The provincial hospital was 110 kilometers away over dirt roads but being July, the French surgeon was on vacation for two months. There was no point in taking the man there. We briefly considered taking him all the way to the Schweitzer Hospital, but that was in Lambarene, over 300 kilometers away over dirt roads. The best solution was Tchibanga, the capital of Nyanga province and 125 kilometers to the west. There was supposed to be a surgeon there.

We told the patient what had to be done. He was not at all happy about going to Tchibanga for it was in the tribal area of the Bapounou people and he was Banzebi. He had no relatives in Tchibanga. He told us he would first have to discuss the matter with his family. That seemed only reasonable until we learned that all of his family were still back in his village. Incredibly, none of them had accompanied him to the hospital.

By this time it was starting to get dark. Someone would either have to drive to the patient's village and bring back some of his family or take the patient there. The trip would be on a back road that had not been worked on for at least five years. The log bridges were rotting and unsafe. We reluctantly decided to drive him to his village ourselves and continue on to Tchibanga from there, although it certainly was not a very direct route.

Becki and Sam's wife, Brenda, watched apprehensively as Sam and I laid the patient on a mattress on the floor in the back of the Land Rover. We didn't know when we'd get back or even if we'd make it to the first village. We kissed them goodbye and disappeared into the dusk. It took half an hour to drive the seven kilometers.

Our arrival in the darkened village drew a crowd. Cars rarely ventured on that road and never at night. When the news got around that we had returned to the village with one of their own, some started wailing, thinking we had brought him home to die. The village elders managed to calm everyone down and asked us to explain what we wanted to do. About fifty people jammed into a bark house ten feet by twenty-five feet. Our unfortunate patient, groaning, was helped to the middle of the floor. He lay on a mat, his great belly mute testimony to the seriousness of the situation.

I did not yet speak Banzebi although I understood some of what they were saying. I explained in French why we needed to take the man to Tchibanga for an operation. A great hubbub ensued as various family members voiced their objections. They were afraid and claimed that they didn't have enough money for the trip. (This was mainly to impress the extended family members so that they would contribute.) Some seemed to think the sorcerer ought to be given another try, but he had already failed. The sorcerer wisely declined.

It had been a very long day for Sam and me and we had hoped to be on our way after only a fifteen-minute delay in the village. There were still another four or five hours of night driving over unfamiliar dirt roads. I did not know anybody in Tchibanga and we had not thought to bring food. After twenty minutes of listening to the discussion, I stepped outside to escape the heat and smell of bodies in the closed room. Sam was admiring the stars. The night sky was like black velvet studded with millions of diamonds. Under normal circumstances it was breathtaking. Tonight it made me feel tired.

"What are they doing in there?" Sam asked, somewhat irritated at the delay. The people did not seem to be too concerned either about the patient's deteriorating condition or about the passage of time.

"They're deciding if they're going to let us take him to Tchibanga and who will give him money so he can eat while he's there," I explained, trying not to show my own frustration. I knew that getting angry would accomplish nothing. We could only entrust ourselves to God for the hours of uncertainty that lay ahead.

Forty-five minutes later the meeting broke up. We were relieved to learn that we would be allowed to continue on with the patient to Tchibanga. His two wives and his children began bringing baskets of pots and pans, food, bedding and clothing out to the car. We arranged the things. Then the patient and one of his wives got in. At last we were ready to pull out.

As I prepared to close the back door, there seemed to be an additional problem. Several women were arguing with the elders. Soon everyone was talking at once. Someone started shouting. The conversation was too rapid for me to understand. Several women started taking things out of the back of the car. The wife who was in the car climbed out. I moved away from the door and asked a young man who spoke French what was happening.

"Well," he said with a faint smile, "they are arguing over which of his two wives gets to go with him. The one who stays home will have to do all the work and the oldest wife decided she did not want to be the one to stay home!" I ground my teeth but said nothing. While time was wasting, they were arguing about which wife would go? Before I was able to say or do something I would probably regret, the other wife climbed into the car, followed by her belongings. Finally we were ready to begin the trip.

It took us two hours driving over the overgrown trail to get out to the main road. By then the car was covered with leaves, sap, impacted insects and mud. Our patient moaned whenever we hit a bump. Around 1 a.m. we found ourselves on a new section of road that was smooth, wide and straight. What a relief to be able to drive eighty kilometers an hour on the packed dirt. But after an hour, the road abruptly changed. Soon we were bouncing over enormous ruts and easing into ditches three feet across and a foot deep. All of a sudden the road ended in a tangle of brush. Either the city of Tchibanga had been swallowed by the jungle or we had missed a turn.

It took us almost an hour to get back to the corner we had missed. At 2 a.m. we asked directions of a man walking along the road and by 3 a.m. we could see the lights of Tchibanga below.

We drove around town for twenty minutes before locating the hospital. There was one nurse on duty for the entire hospital and he was only half sober. He gave our patient a bed and called the doctor. We could hear the doctor scolding the nurse for waking him, but he did tell the nurse to pass a naso-gastric tube to decompress the patient's abdomen. The nurse explained that the doctor would see the patient in the morning.

Sam and I were not happy with the decision, but there was nothing more to do but try to find a place to sleep. The nurse gave us directions to the local Alliance church, the only Protestant church in town. We drove up to the church and parked. As we were arranging our sleeping bags, the pastor appeared and tapped on the car window. I explained to Pastor Joel who we were and why we had come. He insisted that we sleep in his guest room. He awakened the whole family, including six children, and had them clear out a wheelbarrow and shovels from a nearby shed. Clouds of dust billowed out the door and windows as the children hastily swept it out. Two of the older children appeared from nowhere with a double bed and mattress and set it up in the shed. We thanked the pastor and said goodnight. In minutes we were asleep, too tired to care about the multitudes of mosquitoes swirling around our heads.

It was 8:00 a.m. before we even moved. Pastor Joel's wife provided warm water to wash up with, then invited us to eat breakfast with the rest of the family. The table was set with their best dishes and tablecloth. Including the children, we were ten around the small table. As we bowed to give thanks, I noticed something out of the corner of my eye. When the prayer ended, I glanced through an open door to my right into what was obviously the master bedroom. It was a small room. On the cement floor was a blanket. There was no bed or mattress in the room. Suddenly I understood. The pastor and his wife had given complete strangers their own bed in the middle of the night and had spent the rest of the night on the cement floor. Tears filled my eyes. I blinked them back quickly. Nobody seemed to notice.

Breakfast consisted of French bread dipped in hot "coffee," but because the pastor had no coffee, we dipped it into hot water mixed with sweetened condensed milk.

Sam and I checked on our patient before we left for home. The doctor had not yet come to see him, but the tube had helped and already he looked better. We later learned that he did not require surgery and recovered completely, his obstruction probably due to a large tangle of intestinal worms.

As Sam and I drove home, we marveled at God's ways. The kindness we had shown to a sick man had been returned to us by the pastor and his wife. We should have been tired, but our hearts were too full of gratitude to notice.

17

Showdown at the Louetsi

Staging and symbolism play an important part in much of Africa and newcomers, particularly North Americans who often sniff at ceremony, soon learn about it the hard way.

A high school student drowned in the Louetsi River while swimming in the waters below the falls. His body was not found for three days and then only because it floated to the surface, bloated and grotesque. The police were called and they requested that I come down to the river to inspect the body for signs of foul play. Unaware of the significance of the moment, I came dressed in plain clothes. My mission, as I understood it was simple: to establish that the boy had perished by drowning and not by foul play.

The cause of death even in seemingly routine cases is a matter of great importance in Africa. The Gabonese always suspect foul play and consider those who don't to be naive. For the West African, all sicknesses, accidents and misfortunes are caused by people through the spirits which are invisible. The only way to obtain protection is by performing certain acts or owning or wearing a sacred object which is called a fetish. What the Africans do not recognize, however, is the principle which is clearly taught in the Scriptures: that those who enlist the help of spirits will be enslaved by them. The only deliverance from this slavery is through the Name and power of the Lord Jesus Christ. What I failed to understand at the river was that the cause of this young man's death held such significance in their culture and community.

The bloated body had been dragged half out of the water and was beginning to decompose. It smelled as bad as it looked. The police stood a respectful distance away while I examined the body. There were no cuts, fractures, bruises or depressions in the skull. Several fingernails were torn, probably as the victim fought to regain the surface. There were no signs of crocodile bites, but that did not surprise me since there had not been crocodiles reported below the falls in decades. I finished the examination in about 10 minutes, washed my hands in the river and walked up to where the police were making out their report. As I described my findings to the chief, I heard a commotion across the river.

A procession of at least fifty people was approaching the ferry. At the head of the procession marched "Dr." Bayonne. He was gloved, masked and dressed in a green operating gown. His hands were held in the air in front of him like a surgeon ready to enter the operating room. On each side and behind him were the nurses from the Lebamba hospital, in uniform and carrying various instruments. At least thirty men and women followed, accompanied by as many children and dogs. Bayonne stood silently at the river's edge while the ferry crossers hastily maneuvered closer. By now the police were not interested in what I was saying—the real doctor had arrived!

Once the ferry crossed the river, Bayonne strode majestically ashore and approached the body. He did not touch it but circled several times, inspecting it from all sides, his gloved hands still held high. Then, his gaze still fixed on the body, he held out one hand to the nurse holding the stethoscope. The nurse slapped it smartly into his open palm. Almost tenderly he touched the stethoscope to the corpse's chest. He listened for almost a minute, and although everyone knew the boy had been dead for days, they waited with bated breath. Finally, the "doctor" straightened and shook his head. A compassionate murmur ran through the crowd. He turned to the chief of police and explained the cause of death in tones that all could hear. One of his nurses tried to write it all down, scribbling furiously during the entire five-minute discourse.

When the police had no further questions, Bayonne stripped off his gloves and handed them to another nurse. He shook hands all around, gave me a casual glance and recrossed the river along with his entourage. It had been a marvelous performance.

Bayonne certainly knew how to inspire faith in his patients. I began to understand that if I wanted my patients to follow my orders after they returned home, I would have to help them to believe in me. Furthermore, only if I succeeded in inspiring them to place their trust in God would they live forever. My first task, then, was not to establish a program—it was to win the confidence and respect of the people.

18

The Prefet's Wife

I awoke to the sound of my name being called over the CB radio.

"Yes, this is the doctor," I answered. "What is it?"

"The mayor of Lebamba is at the Louetsi with his wife." I knew that if the mayor wanted to cross the Louetsi at 5:00 a.m. something was seriously wrong.

A mayor in Gabon is called a prefet (pronounced pray-fay) and he is an important government official. I dressed hastily, got into the truck and started down the hill. It had been raining steadily all night and the road was very slick. The last 100 yards to the ferry were covered with about two inches of mud so slippery it was difficult to even stand. I decided to leave the truck at the top of the hill with the lights on and walk down. I could see the prefet and his wife climb into the long canoe on the opposite shore. Having crossed the river, the prefet's wife stepped out first, helped

136

by her husband and another woman. She was very weak and feverish and we had to carry her up the hill to the car. As we drove to the hospital, I asked what had happened.

The prefet was very angry, but did explain that his wife was due to have a baby and after running a high fever for four hours the day before, she had gone into labor. He had taken her to the government hospital in Lebamba to see the French doctor who had hospitalized her and treated her for malaria. Her labor had seemed to be progressing normally, but her fever rose alarmingly to 105 degrees Fahrenheit and stayed there. The prefet felt that the doctor did not realize the seriousness of his wife's condition and finally asked him to transfer her to our hospital. The doctor reluctantly agreed, but it was the middle of the night, and rather than take the prefet and his wife to the river himself, he sent for the hospital chauffeur and went back to bed. By the time someone found the chauffeur it was four hours later, the prefet was furious and the prefet's wife was in serious condition.

It was still dark as we drove up the hill to the hospital. We carried the barely conscious woman into the delivery room and examined her. Her temperature was still 105 degrees, her blood pressure was falling and her pulse was weak. The baby was nearly ready to come. As the nurses started an IV, I asked the prefet's wife to push as hard as she could. With her remaining strength, she pushed the baby out.

It was too late. The baby had died several hours earlier from an intrauterine infection. Within minutes, the woman went into shock and lost consciousness. For the next two hours we did everything we knew to save her life. Several times we prayed for wisdom and asked God to spare her. At last, her blood pressure stabilized, she regained consciousness and we were able to move her to a private room under close nursing supervision.

Despite her improvement over the next two days her condition remained critical and we did not have the broad spectrum antibiotics she needed to control the infection. Since we did not have an Intensive Care Unit, I felt that as soon as her condition was stable we should transfer her to Libreville by plane. Her husband agreed.

My car was the most comfortable vehicle available, so we arranged for one of the missionary nurses to drive them to Mouila, 110 kilometers away, to catch the plane to Libreville. The prefet made an unusual request as we made preparations to leave: he wanted someone from our hospital to accompany them all the way to Libreville. I was reluctant to have one of my staff go, but when he explained that our personnel were the only ones who seemed to care about his wife, I agreed to let a nurse go as far as Mouila. Before they left, I asked the prefet if I could pray for his wife and for their trip. He immediately agreed and I prayed the simplest, most direct evangelistic message I have ever prayed. When I finished, the prefet wiped his eyes. His voice trembled as he shook my hand goodbye.

"No one has ever treated us as kindly as you people," he said softly. "We will never forget it."

His wife spent nearly a month convalescing in the hospital in Libreville. It was about six months later that she visited us at Bongolo. I did not recognize the sharply dressed, attractive woman who greeted me. To my embarrassment, she had to introduce herself to me. I think she was secretly pleased that I did not recognize her. She seemed very happy to be back and greeted all of the staff at the hospital, thanking them for saving her life.

She and her husband became enthusiastic supporters of the hospital ministry but neither one has invited Christ into his or her life. Their oldest son, however, decided to follow Christ and was baptized.

The prefet was reassigned to another post and before he left I paid them a visit. I gave them each a Christian book and a tract on how to receive the gift of eternal life. As we sat in their living room, the wife told me that she remembered the morning when she nearly died and she recalled that I drove her to the hospital. Barely conscious as we drove up the hill, she had looked out the window and seen a white light shining over the hospital. A feeling of inexpressible peace filled her soul.

"In that moment, I believed in your God," she told me. "I could feel that He was there and that He would help me."

I thought back to that night. I never saw anything shining over the hospital, but I don't doubt that the prefet's wife saw something supernatural there.

We continue to trust that through the care and kindness shown at the Bongolo Evangelical Hospital that this Gabonese couple will find Christ.

19

As Small as a Mustard Seed

The room was darkened, but there was enough light coming through the window of the mud-plastered hospital room to see the young Gabonese nursing student lying comatose on the bed. From a bottle above his bed, fluid dripped into a vein in his arm. In the tropical heat his body was shiny with perspiration. From time to time a young woman wiped the sweat off his face with a towel.

There were other family members in the room and they watched his steady breathing in silence, hopelessness written on their faces. His older brother, also a nurse, stood by his bed for long hours, saying nothing.

Frederic was in a deep coma and the outlook for him was not good. Three days earlier I had started him on a treatment for filaria. His body was filled with the tiny hairlike worms that crawl under the skin and cause intense itching. He had begged for the treatment to eradicate them.

I warned him of the dangers and of the need for extreme caution. He seemed to understand, but still wanted the treatment. The first and second days after taking minuscule doses he experienced the usual initial symptoms of fatigue and heaviness. On the third day, unknown to me, he began having severe, unrelenting headaches. That evening he took the third dose and went to bed. In the morning he did not wake up.

Frederic's fellow students brought him to the hospital where I began a course of drugs to decrease the swelling of his brain and other organs. He ran a high fever and his condition only worsened by the hour.

As we went about our work that day at the hospital a great black cloud hovered over us. Instead of the usual smiles there was heaviness. Uppermost in our minds was a similar case we had seen a year before. A pastor's daughter, on the same medication, had gone into a coma that lasted for weeks. When the elders of the church anointed her with oil and prayed for her, she came out of the coma, but remained severely paralyzed and unable to talk. Realizing the extent of her paralysis, she gave up the will to live. A month later, anxious to be with her Savior and having suffered terribly, she died.

I was appalled. I had promised myself after her death that it would never happen again at our hospital. And now, in spite of what I thought were adequate precautions, it had happened again. As I looked down at Frederic's swollen and feverish body I silently asked God to heal him and to spare him from what had happened to the pastor's daughter.

Standing by his bed, I sensed God speaking to me. The meaning of what He said was clear: "If *all* of you pray and believe, I will heal him. If you will not *all* pray, I will do nothing. This has happened to show you My power." In the same moment I was filled with self-doubt. Perhaps I was just thinking what I wanted to believe. In the end I knew that God was challenging me to move out in faith.

I looked around the room at Frederic's fellow students. They were young and immature Christians. Most had never attended a prayer meeting. How could I get them to pray and really believe? None had ever seen a person healed and neither had any of our Gabonese nurses. Meanwhile, despite the best treatment I could devise, Frederic's condition continued to deteriorate.

As I looked into the faces of the students the Lord again spoke to me, "I want them to see My power and believe in Me." With inward reservations I invited everyone to a prayer meeting that night at the church.

By 8:00 p.m. about twenty of us were gathered. I opened my Bible to Mark 9:23 and read aloud the words of Jesus: "Everything is possible for him who believes." I looked around at the young faces. They seemed to be saying, "Really?

Everything?" Or was it the questioning of my
own heart?

I then turned to Matthew 9:29 and read: "According to your faith will it be done to you." If
only it could be true for Frederic! One by one we
began to pray. Some prayed with hesitancy, others with great fervor.

After some time I stood and read again the
words of Jesus, this time from Matthew 17:20
and 21: "I tell you the truth, if you have faith as
small as a mustard seed, you can say to this
mountain, 'Move from here to there' and it will
move. Nothing will be impossible for you."

That verse seemed to instill true hope in our
hearts. There was a longing to believe and not
doubt that God would heal him. In my own heart
there came the conviction that because we were
praying, God would do as He had promised: He
would heal Frederic! Now many began to entreat
the Lord for faith to believe for Frederic's healing.

As it grew late some left, but many stayed, alter-
nately praying, singing and sharing Scriptures. At
midnight, weary from the day's work, we said our
goodnights and went home to bed, certain that
God would heal Frederic that very night.

In the morning as we started the hospital
rounds there was an air of expectancy; but when
we entered Frederic's room it vanished. His
condition had not changed. His mother sat
weeping in a corner of the room, her tears falling
silently onto the floor.

As I tried to take refuge in studying Frederic's chart, the Lord once again spoke to me. This time He brought to my mind one of the verses I had read the night before: "According to your faith will it be done to you" (Matthew 9:29). The Lord wanted us to believe in spite of what we saw.

I admonished those in the room, "Let's not stop believing that God will heal Frederic! God wants all of us to believe—not just me or a few of the missionary nurses, but all of us who prayed! This is not the time to wonder if maybe it isn't God's will! This is the time to insist before the Lord that we want Him to heal Frederic!"

That afternoon Frederic awoke from his coma. Those who had nurtured in their hearts the mustard seed of faith were not surprised, but rejoiced. "It's because we prayed that God healed him!" one student exulted.

But the healing was only partial. Frederic was awake, yes, but he could not talk. He could only walk with two people holding him up. We had asked God for total healing. We continued to pray for him.

Three days later I brought a very shaky Frederic to the Bible study we held in our home every Friday night for our male nurses and nursing students. After the Bible study we laid hands on Frederic and prayed for his complete recovery.

His improvement during the following week was dramatic. He began to talk and soon was able to walk unassisted. But because his eyes could not focus, he still could neither read nor write.

The following Friday night Frederic asked us to lay hands on him again and pray, this time for his eyes and hands so that he could read and write and resume his classes. The students prayed boldly for their classmate.

Within six weeks Frederic recovered completely. Able to read and write again, he caught up on his studies and resumed working at the hospital. He is a living, walking testimony to the power of God and the importance of unified, persistent prayers of faith.

20

The River

A major river in the African rain forest is a formidable geographical obstacle. Living in developed countries where we cross two or three bridges on the way to the supermarket, we tend not to even think about bridges. But in Africa where bridges are precious and few, a river is a force to be reckoned with.

The Louetsi River is a case in point. During the dry season months of June through September, the river shrinks down to a width of only thirty yards, with a maximum depth of perhaps eight or ten feet. But in the rainy season, particularly during the peak months of November and March, the river rises some eighteen feet and can swell to a width of 200 feet or more. When the Louetsi is low, the thirty-foot high Bongolo Falls flow softly across a thirty-yard span. When it is high, the falls thunder awesomely across a fifty-yard precipice, spewing great white plumes of spray.

The simplest way to cross the Louetsi is in an African dugout canoe. The canoes are usually made from an entire okoume (pronounced o-KOO-may) tree because okoume wood takes several years to rot, even when continuously wet. It is a delight to watch one or two expert paddlers skim a small, two-man canoe up, down and across the river. The passengers show little concern that the water line is only one-half inch below the top edge of the canoe's sides! A little injudicious leaning, a moment off-balance and water pours in. I have seen a skilled canoeist fill a ten-foot canoe to the top with wet sand, leaving only a quarter inch of canoe above the waterline, and then paddle it across a fast-flowing river without letting a drop of water inside.

Large canoes are heavy and awkward to control. To make a really large canoe practical, the early missionaries rigged a cable across the river so that an operator standing on the prow could pull the canoe across, hand over hand. In this way, depending on the size of the canoe, twenty or even thirty people could be transported at once.

To cross a thirty-foot dugout canoe holding on to a one-inch steel cable is not as easy as it looks, especially if the canoe is heavily loaded and the river is high. For years the Lebamba mayor has paid two local men to take people across in the large canoe. When they are sober, they are reliable crossers, but when they are drunk or when an overconfident volunteer decides to cross the canoe, interesting things can happen.

If the crosser misjudges the current or the weight of his load, the current pulls the canoe out from under him and he must either hold onto the cable and let the canoe go, or go with the canoe and let go of the cable. If you're watching from the security of the shore, the result is sadly funny. The passengers send up a mournful cry which soon changes to a babble of disbelief. As the canoe drifts slowly downriver and out of sight the human sounds of outrage and disbelief fade away. Somewhere downstream it eventually bumps into the shore and the frustrated passengers clamber ashore. To return to civilization they must thrash their way along the bank and through the jungle until they encounter a path.

The logical solution to all this would be to build a bridge. Given the depth and width of the Louetsi River during the peak of the rainy seasons and given Bongolo's remote location, building a bridge large enough for cars would be a logistic nightmare and very expensive. Since the government has never considered Bongolo important enough to merit a bridge and since missionaries have hesitated to ask their friends and supporters for two million dollars to build one, a bridge has never been built.

Even if some philanthropist were to donate two million dollars, the problem of finding someone capable of engineering and building the bridge would persist. Bridge-building companies simply do not exist in West Africa.

The cheapest and simplest way to cross cars and trucks over the Louetsi is by pontoon ferry. All three of the ferries that have been built in Bongolo were made by missionaries. I was told that the first ferry was made from fifty-five-gallon steel drums lashed together and topped with a platform. In the 1960s a determined missionary named Don Dirks welded together an open-hulled ferry with ramps that could be raised or lowered. Cars drove down into the hull. Subsequent missionaries added side pontoons so that the ferry could carry two cars at a time.

The ferry's main weakness was its tendency to collect rainwater. Before it could be safely used after a heavy rain, it had to be pumped out. When we arrived in Bongolo in 1977, this ferry was in operation. Newly arrived and still accustomed to bridges, we did not appreciate it for what it was—a Cadillac among Bongolo ferries. It served us well until 1981.

Unless you have lived in either the Amazon basin or in West Equatorial Africa, it is hard to imagine how much water can fall out of the sky in the space of a few hours. I once measured four inches of rainfall in one hour. Such was the rainstorm that nearly drowned Bongolo in 1981.

That afternoon while it continued to rain "goats and camels," at least six inches of water collected in the bottom of the ferry. During the storm, two high school students decided to cross the river on the ferry. The large canoe was on the opposite side of the river and the paid crossers had gone home to get out of the rain. The students did not know that it was very important to turn the ferry when crossing to protect it from the full force of the current. This was especially critical if the ferry was heavily loaded or, in this case, full of water. The students pulled mightily to get the low-riding craft out into the middle of the river and when the full force of the current hit the ferry, water poured into the hull. In less than a minute, hundreds of missionary man-hours and several thousand dollars worth of steel, cable and lumber were forever lost. The ferry sank. The students managed to swim to safety. All efforts to salvage the ferry proved fruitless.

It took two years to build a new one. In the interim we used an old logging road to get out to the main road. Where before it had taken ten minutes to drive to Lebamba, now it took an hour.

Daan Bijl, one of our Dutch missionaries, made a new ferry by welding four steel pontoons from sheet metal, bolting them together and attaching a wooden platform on top. This ferry was lighter and easier to use, but supported only one car at a time.

One day Becki and I drove onto the new ferry on our way to visit one of our satellite dispensaries. I noticed that the end of the ferry sticking out into the river was quite low. Obviously, one of the pontoons was full of water. We had crossed before with one pontoon full of water, so it didn't concern me much. What I did not know was that a second pontoon was also punctured and full of water.

The weight of the truck pushed the pontoons lower into the water. I didn't realize that the two pontoons closest to the shore were resting on the bottom, keeping the ferry from sinking as low as it should have. The Bongolo high school let out for lunch just as we pulled onto the ferry and about twenty students ran down and clambered on. I was not too happy but figured the ferry could handle the load.

Since the ferry was resting on the bottom, the students had to help me pull on the cable to get us moving. As we lost the support of the river bottom and moved into deep water, the ferry sank until the planks we were standing on were covered by about an inch of water. Before we could turn back, the strong current caught us, pushing the ferry under until there was nothing visible out in the middle of the river except twenty-two screaming people standing up to their knees in water and holding on to the truck. The pressure of the current pushed the ferry deeper and deeper and, as the water rose to the bottom of the doors on the truck, I realized that at any moment it would float away. I wondered what it would be like to spend the rest of our term without a vehicle.

Becki and I stood hanging on to the truck not knowing what to do. Without a $20,000 vehicle to worry about, the high school students began abandoning ship, jumping into the water and swimming for the nearest shore. After about fifteen of them had jumped off, the ferry struggled to surface. Twenty feet from shore the planks beneath our feet finally broke the surface and, pulling on the cable, we made it to the other side. Fortunately, all of the students reached shore safely although many lost their notebooks, papers and pens. To this day I do not understand why the ferry cable did not break under the strain. Perhaps the Lord sent one of His angels to hold onto it. The next year Daan Bijl went on furlough, leaving me in charge of the ferry. Because I didn't know how to weld, when the inevitable pontoon puncture occurred, I had to go begging for help from the Lebamba government officials. Technically, they were responsible to maintain the ferry. Two weeks passed before a work crew from Lebamba showed up to begin repairs. I showed them how to remove the pontoon and they hauled it away to Lebamba on our trailer.

A week later I stopped by the garage in Lebamba to see how it was coming. Because they didn't have any welding rods, nothing had been done. I sent some over from the mission. Another week went by before I had a chance to check on their progress. They showed me the repaired pontoon, but they had no paint. I sent some over from the mission.

In the meantime a second pontoon sprung a leak so it was taken to Lebamba, too. A week later there was no sign of the repaired pontoons, so I made another trip to see what was happening. After an hour I managed to find the man in charge. He explained that the second pontoon was so rusty they would have to replace the entire bottom panel. Unfortunately, they had no steel plating, so he would have to go to Libreville to get some. He was planning to leave in the morning. I commended him for his thoroughness and persistence, trying not to concentrate on the fact that it was taking them weeks to do what Daan usually did in a day. It had been five weeks since we had been able to use the ferry.

About this same time I was having problems with the Mission canoe. This was a four-man dugout canoe that we used to cross the river twice a week to service the hydroelectric plant and water pump. The canoe was beginning to rot and it leaked badly. In order to cross the river, I first had to bail out the canoe. I then rowed like a mad man, arriving on the far shore with four inches of water sloshing around my ankles. What with the leaking canoe, the broken down ferry and my regular medical duties and emergencies at the hospital, I sometimes felt like I was drowning.

Four weeks after leaving for Libreville, the Lebamba official responsible for repairing the ferry returned. He had been delayed by "illness," but had nevertheless managed to locate some steel plating. Within two weeks he repaired the pontoon and put the ferry back together. Eleven weeks after the original leak, the ferry was again operational. One either soon learns patience in Africa or gets a bad case of ulcers!

Those who cross the Louetsi by ferry on a regular basis inevitably develop a love-hate relationship with it. When the ferry was not working, I appreciated it, but after it was repaired, we soon took it for granted.

On more occasions than I care to remember I arrived at the river late at night, only to find both the ferry and the canoe tied on the opposite shore. When this happened, there was little choice but to wade into the water, then holding on to the cable, cross hand over hand to the other side. The first 10 times or so I did this I was terrified, thinking of what could happen if my hands slipped from the cable. I imagined myself paddling in inky-black water, feeling the prickly leaves scraping my face as I pulled myself on shore, vines dangling down my back and across my neck. (One's imagination works very well on dark nights!) Once, as I reached midstream, I thought of a four-foot-long water snake I had seen at that crossing. I gradually learned to cross the river without thinking, concentrating only on putting one hand in front of the other until my feet touched ground on the other side.

The most memorable experience with the ferry occurred one night when I was on it alone. Earlier in the day I had noticed that the loop of cable holding the ferry from going downstream was badly frayed. It had been that way for a month. I thought to myself, *If that cable ever breaks, the ferry will simply drift away downriver where no one will ever be able to recover it.*

Ten hours later and bone-weary from my travels, I crossed the Louetsi alone in the dark, thankful that the ferry had at least been on my side of the river. Using the cable loop, I turned the ferry slightly so that the current would take it across the river without my having to pull on the hand cable. My mind was on the pleasant prospect of a shower and a hot supper when I heard a gentle metallic "pop" near the cable loop. It had parted at the spot where it had frayed and even as I watched, the end slithered away. I grabbed the frayed end of the cable just before it passed through the last connecting pulley. That cable was the only thing keeping me, my truck and the ferry from certain disaster somewhere downstream.

I did not know if I could hold on. Praying for strength, I planted my feet and held on for dear life. The ferry had started to swing away as the cable parted, but when I grabbed the end, the full weight of its momentum dragged against my hands. They were being pulled towards the pulley. With a strength born of desperation and the help of an invisible hand, my hands stopped only inches from disaster.

After what seemed like an hour, but was probably only one or two minutes, the ferry slid out of the current and the pontoons scraped on the bottom. Once again, by God's mercy, I had been spared.

21

No Family—
New Family

The only sounds in the jungle cemetery were made by the shovels clanking and the clumps of dirt hitting the coffin as we filled the grave. It was very hot work. The mourners packed the dirt into a neat mound over the grave, scolding one of the men who started to pack the dirt with his feet instead of his hands. One of them placed a manioc plant at the head to mark the grave.

The dead man had been a patient at the hospital. He had liver cancer and despite our best ministrations he steadily weakened. Day after day the chaplain spoke to him about his need to make a commitment to follow Christ, but the man hesitated, putting off the decision, hoping for a miracle.

When he first came we thought he had someone with him to cook his food and care for him. Fearing that we would send him away if he didn't, he lied, insisting that a family member was with him. His fellow patients shared their food with typical African generosity. When he had no money to pay the $2-a-day hospital fee, we began to wonder. Only when he weakened and had to be transferred to a private room did we discover that he was alone.

One day the Lord told me to go talk to him. I had been busy with scheduled operations and rounds and did not finish with surgery until nearly 1 o'clock. I was tired. I knew the man's French was poor so I would have to speak to him in his more difficult native tongue. Perhaps he wouldn't understand me, I reasoned. Perhaps he would be too weak. But the Lord had spoken to me for a reason and I knew I must obey. I forced my unwilling feet toward his door.

He lay quietly on the bed, emaciated, jaundiced from the cancer, but wide awake. It was clear he could not live much longer. Despite his obvious weakness, he responded warmly to my greeting. I sat on the edge of his bed and asked about his family. With sorrow in his voice he told me that his children and relatives were all in the capital city of Libreville, 540 kilometers to the north. He had sent word to them that he was ill and that he needed their help, but as yet, no one had come. He felt totally abandoned.

"You know you are dying and that I can do no more to help you," I said gently.

"Yes."

"Are you ready to meet God?" I asked.

"No, I don't think so," he answered after a pause.

"You know you will soon be face-to-face with the God who made you. Have you thought of why He should let you into His house?"

He did not know why, but he wanted to know. And so, speaking haltingly in his language I explained God's plan of salvation through Jesus Christ. When I invited him to ask Christ into his heart by praying, he accepted immediately. His prayer was somewhat confused so I called Pastor Luc to talk with him again. This time he prayed with more understanding, asking God to forgive him for his sin, expressing confidence that Jesus Christ was God's only Son and that He alone could save him.

Late that night the man lapsed into a coma and died. Two hours later five members of his family arrived from Libreville after traveling all day. They were beside themselves with grief. As is the custom in West Africa, they threw themselves to the ground, poured dirt on their heads and wailed and wept all night long. Their sorrow was compounded by feelings of guilt that they had waited so long to respond to their father's pleas for help.

Early in the morning Pastor Luc offered to help them make the burial arrangements. When they indicated that they wanted to pay for a coffin, he hired a carpenter to build one. When he told them that we had already prepared the grave, they were speechless.

"Why do you do all this for us?" one of them finally asked.

"Because we are God's children," Pastor Luc
answered simply. "God commands us to love one
another."

The family wrapped the body in new sheets
and placed it in the coffin. The carpenter stood
respectfully nearby with a hammer and some
nails and when the family was ready, nailed the
lid onto the coffin. We loaded it into the back of
my truck and took it to the graveside. Pastor Luc
addressed the group.

"This man came to us sick, with no money and
with no family. Because we are God's children
we took him in and cared for him as best we
could. But before he died, he found a new family—the family of God. He invited Jesus Christ
into his heart and became one of God's own
children. Today he is in heaven with God. If any
of you were to die today, would you go to
heaven?" There was an uncomfortable silence.

Finally, the oldest daughter answered. "Because
of the kindness you have shown to my father and
to us, I know that what you say is true, Pastor. We
have never experienced such kindness from
strangers. We can see that God is in your hearts.
But now we are too troubled to decide such a
thing." Pastor Luc shook his head slightly.

"Do not wait too long before you decide. God
is speaking to you right now. Tomorrow you may
not think about Him anymore." He paused for a
moment, but when they only stared at the cof-

fin, he nodded and prayed, thanking God for the salvation of the man whose body was about to be buried.

As we filled in the grave, my heart was heavy that these people would return to Libreville not knowing Christ. But for the man in the grave—he would live forever. "By this will all men know that you are my disciples, if you love one another" (John 13:35).

22

Veronica

Late one night just several weeks before Christmas, I was awakened by someone pounding on the front door. We had no telephones or CB radios at that time, so when there were emergencies during the night the nurses had to walk the half-mile up the hill to my house and pound on the door until I answered. When I opened the door, I saw a middle-aged man holding a smoking kerosene lantern. The flickering light cast shadows across his anxious face. In broken French he explained that his daughter had suddenly fallen ill. I was surprised to see that even at night the man wore a battered felt hat.

As we drove down the hill to the hospital the father explained his daughter's symptoms. It sounded to me like a severe case of malaria. We pulled up in front of the darkened mud-brick ward. The headlights scattered a group of the ever-present goats that had been sleeping on the front steps. The windows were tightly shuttered to keep out the mosquitoes and the air inside the building was heavy.

Veronica lay on a brightly colored cloth her mother had spread on the bare boards of the bed. Although she was only about nine years old, because she was thin she looked older. I surmised that she must have been ill for several weeks. Her dark eyes looked at me solemnly. While the other patients in the room watched with interest, I examined the little girl. In the dim light I could see nothing wrong with her, except that she had a fever of 104 degrees and her liver was slightly enlarged. Many African children have an enlarged liver because of chronic malaria, so I was not overly concerned. I treated her for malaria and instructed Norbert to give her aspirin to control the fever. I said goodnight and returned home, wondering why Veronica's father seemed so concerned. Such fevers are common for children.

As I climbed between the clean sheets, the cool night air flowed through the screened window. I was unable, however, to sleep. The more I thought about Veronica, the more uneasy I felt about my diagnosis. It did not help that her father had thanked me with an expression of absolute trust. I found it unsettling.

The next day Veronica was worse and for the next three to four days the high fever persisted. I started her on antibiotics, thinking perhaps she had typhoid fever, but still she did not improve. Although the nurses and I were busy with outpatient clinics and with about thirty other patients in the ward, Veronica's struggle to live became the focus of everyone's attention. It was clear that unless we were able to do something soon, she would die. A feeling of gloom settled over us. As Veronica's condition worsened, her father no longer looked at me with trust. I did not share with him my utter frustration that I did not even have the equipment to take a simple x-ray.

My thoughts turned to the Christmas we were trying to celebrate. It was our first Christmas in Africa, but it did not seem like Christmas. Our artificial tree, decorated with colored lights and shining ornaments looked awkward and out of place. Although we had attended colorful and enthusiastic Christmas celebrations in the African church, we remained spectators and not participants. Our joy over the coming of Christ seemed largely an intellectual exercise.

That week, during our Wednesday night prayer meeting, we prayed for a long time that God would heal Veronica and that she and her family would come to know Christ through our efforts. We also asked God to give us wisdom.

Several nights later I was awakened again by shouting and pounding on the front door. Once more Veronica's father stood outside the door, this time accompanied by one of the African nurses. As tears streamed down his face, he pleaded with me to come save his daughter. She had suddenly begun to breathe with difficulty. The nurse confirmed that the situation was indeed urgent, so I threw on my clothes and raced down the hill to the hospital. The other patients were awake and watching as the little girl gasped. As two nurses held up lanterns for light, I examined her and discovered that the right side of her chest had filled with fluid.

I needed a sterile chest tube to drain out the fluid that had collapsed her lung, but the supplies and equipment we had ordered from Europe and the United States had not yet come. After a frantic search, one of the nurses discovered an old, yellowed naso-gastric tube. As we boiled it along with some instruments, I explained to Veronica's mother and father what I had to do to save their daughter.

The result was pandemonium. Up to this point, Veronica's mother had calmed and encouraged her daughter, but now she began wailing and throwing herself on the floor in the traditional manner of mourning a loved one's death.

Realizing that the girl's life hung in the balance, I whisked her into the curtained treatment room and lay her on the table. In the dim lantern light, with two nurses holding her down on the table and her father struggling to keep his frantic wife from getting in the door, I injected a local anesthetic, made a small incision into the right side of Veronica's chest between two ribs and inserted the tube. Nearly two quarts of dark brown fluid drained out of her side.

Veronica's mother stopped wailing and stared in amazement. No physician ever had a more appreciative audience. As more and more liquid poured out, the other patients crowded around the door, murmuring in wonder. Veronica's breathing gradually became more regular.

I concluded that Veronica might have had a large amoebic abscess of the liver that had ruptured into her chest, although I was never able to prove that diagnosis. We left the drain in for a week and treated her with appropriate antibiotics. Eventually she recovered.

Before she left the hospital, Veronica gave her heart to Christ. Her father and mother never did become Christians, but whenever I met her father in town, he would remove his battered hat and proclaim to everyone within earshot that I was the doctor God had sent to save his daughter from certain death. With each telling the story seemed to get better, but since God got most of the credit, I didn't object. As a result of Veronica's recovery, our fame spread far and wide. The hospital was inundated with patients. Most of them came believing I could cure anything if I set my mind to it. At times when I expressed surprise at their faith in my ability, they would respond, "Oh, your God will show you what to do. After all, He does it for you all the time!" In the face of such faith, what else could I do but carry on?

Veronica's recovery and conversion also lifted the cloud of gloom from our Christmas celebrations. It left us with a deeper understanding of the joy that Christmas brings. Without mountains of presents, the beautiful shopping malls, the lights and decorations, and even without our families, we experienced the first of many warm and wonderful Christmases in Africa. Our joy did not come from partying, nor from the few traditional trappings we had managed to bring with us. It came instead from helping people in great need to regain physical health and find spiritual wholeness in the Christ of Christmas.

23

Lebongo's Wives

The voice calling my name over the CB radio jarred me to consciousness. I stumbled out of bed and into the dimly lit living room to turn down the volume before the noise wakened everyone in the house. It was midnight. I had been asleep for about an hour. I knew that if I didn't answer, the night-duty nurse would continue to call.

"Hello, this is the doctor," I answered. "What do you want?"

"Mister Lebongo Antoine brought his wife in tonight. She's very ill and he wants you to come down right now to see her."

Little did he know that those words fanned into flame a few smoldering coals that I had nurtured in my heart for years. Five years before I had shot and killed one of Lebongo Antoine's goats near the hospital. It was Lebongo, who in a drunken rage, had vowed to get revenge by harming my children. Nothing ever came of his threat, but now the memory of it came back to me like a flood. I was not in the mood to go out of my way for either him or his wife.

"What kind of illness does she have?" I asked. I wasn't going to go down unless the nurse could convince me that someone was going to die if I didn't.

"Well, her abdomen hurts very badly," he answered.

"How long?"

"Since yesterday." Yesterday! And now, at midnight, Mr. Lebongo has decided to bring her to the hospital. It probably was his way of getting even. Well, I wasn't going to play his game.

"How are her vital signs?" I asked suspiciously. The nurse recited them over the CB radio. Everything sounded normal. She could certainly wait until morning.

The nurse was not happy with my decision, especially since he would have to explain it to Lebongo. Since Lebongo drank heavily every evening and would be his usual abusive self, that wouldn't be pleasant. I crawled back into bed.

But I could not sleep. After about twenty minutes I sat up on the edge of the bed. It was no use. I knew when the Lord was unhappy with me and I knew he was ordering me to the hospital. I dressed and drove the kilometer down the hill.

Seeing Lebongo and smelling the alcohol vapors that surrounded him like a cloud brought the goat incident back as though it had been yesterday. With the Lord prompting me I was able to greet Lebongo as though nothing had ever happened between us. He responded with a smile that did not reach his eyes and introduced me to his wife. She was not the gracious Christian woman I had remembered. Seeing my confusion he explained that this woman was his second wife. Her name was Brigitte.

Brigitte looked to be about twenty years old. She lay in bed in a fetal position, moaning softly. She had been sick with continuous lower abdominal pain and nausea for two days. I examined her and decided that she either had a pelvic infection or an extrauterine pregnancy that had ruptured. A pregnancy test was negative, her vital signs were stable and she was not anemic. I decided to start her on intravenous fluids and antibiotics for the more likely diagnosis of pelvic infection. I gave her a shot for pain, instructed the nurses to check her vital signs hourly for the rest of the night and went home.

The next morning she felt better. Lebongo's first wife Martha was caring for Brigitte and her love and concern for her younger rival was touching. I knew that as a Christian she had probably not wanted her husband to take a second wife. As I left the ward, Martha followed me.

"Dr. David," she called after me, "please, if you have time, talk to Brigitte about Jesus. She is not a believer and I am very concerned about her." I could not suppress a smile.

"Why do you care so much about your rival?" I asked.

"Doctor, you know I have prayed for ten years for my husband's salvation. He knows the Jesus way is right, but he does not want to give up his women and his drinking. When he took Brigitte as his second wife, I decided to win her to Christ by praying for her and showing her that I love her. When she becomes a believer, he will have two Christian wives praying for him!" Her faith and logic left me momentarily speechless.

"I promise you I will speak to her about Jesus," I finally answered. She flashed me a brilliant smile. Martha was an attractive woman and she was especially beautiful when she laughed.

Late that same afternoon I stopped by to check on Brigitte's progress. The pain had returned. Her lower abdomen seemed slightly distended and she looked pale. A repeat blood test showed that she was losing blood from somewhere. She agreed to let me take her to the operating room for a diagnostic pelvic needle puncture.

Surprisingly, the needle puncture was negative for blood, but I decided to operate anyway. Her husband's blood matched hers and he immediately donated a unit. Brigitte was very fearful as we gave her a spinal anesthetic and scrubbed her abdomen for surgery. The sight of her husband's blood dripping into her arm only heightened her fear.

I leaned over the anesthesia screen and told her I was going to pray. She nodded jerkily in agreement, certain she was going to die. "Father," I prayed, "please help us now as we operate on

Brigitte. Give us the wisdom and the skill we need to deal with what we find. Help Brigitte to recover completely and without complication after the operation. Above all, Lord Jesus, help Brigitte to learn to trust in you. Amen."

I looked over at Brigitte after my prayer. She managed a weak smile.

When we opened her lower abdomen we found about a quart of fresh blood mixed with old, clotted blood. I located the source of the bleeding: a ruptured fallopian tube pregnancy.

The next day I explained to Brigitte that had I not come down to examine her at midnight and started her on intravenous fluids she would probably have gone into shock during the night and died. She was either extremely lucky or God had protected her from a catastrophic hemorrhage. "Perhaps," I continued, "God is warning you to get right with Him." She looked thoughtful but said nothing. Martha beamed her approval. Lebongo looked uncomfortable.

A week later Brigitte was discharged from the hospital. Somewhat to Lebongo's irritation the illness bound Brigitte and Martha together like sisters. About six months later Brigitte decided to follow Jesus too. Just as Martha had hoped, Lebongo Antoine now had two wives who were working and praying to bring him to the Savior.

24

Nearly Lynched

Only the courageous, the dedicated, the uninformed or the truly determined travel to West Africa. It is not that West Africa is so dangerous—it is just so costly, inconvenient, unpredictable and other-worldly that few strangers have any reason to come. The jungles of Gabon so effectively conceal the large populations of elephants, wild buffalo, gorillas, chimpanzees, monkeys and other animals that those tourists who ignore their travel agents' advice and visit Gabon anyway are usually disappointed.

Westerners come to Gabon for only three reasons: to make money, to visit Dr. Albert Schweitzer's hospital or to accomplish a scientific or benevolent mission. In each case the success of the individual depends on his or her ability and willingness to learn.

Some of the best learners I have encountered in Gabon are medical students. Since 1977 a number of American young people have visited our hospital for short periods of time. We have developed four requirements for these students: they must be followers of Jesus Christ; they must be in the fourth year of medical school; they must pay all their own expenses; and they must be able to speak and understand at least some French.

Although most of our students have found their African experience enjoyable, some have not. One, whom I shall call Steve, faced a tragedy that challenged his faith and reminded all of us that our ability to live and work in Africa ultimately depends on God.

Steve's wife accompanied him to Gabon and their six weeks with us were happy ones. Steve did not speak French and while this limited his ability to function independently at the hospital, it did not hide his affection for the Gabonese people. Our African nurses remember him to this day for his hard work, his interest in them personally and his sensitivity. We were all sorry to see them go, but since he was on his last elective as a medical student, he had to get back to the States to graduate.

Shortly before they left, a missionary from another station invited them to ride with her to Libreville. The trip is 540 kilometers and takes ten to twelve hours of hard driving. Only the last ninety kilometers of the road were in good condition at the time. Once over the worst, Steve volunteered to drive the rest of the way.

By that time, the sun was low in the western sky and directly into their eyes. The road was straight and smooth and while most drivers drove at l00 kilometers per hour, Steve chose to drive between sixty and eighty.

Down the road a bit Steve saw a car parked on the far side of the road. A group of people stood around the rear of the car talking. As Steve approached, a young woman suddenly decided to cross the road. Unable to turn either to the right or the left, he could only slam on the brakes. It was over in an instant. The front of the pickup hit the woman squarely in the back and threw her about thirty feet.

In most countries in Africa, travelers are advised not to stop if their car hits a pedestrian. In Gabon, even the police advise the driver to continue without stopping until he can get to the nearest police station to report the incident. To ignore this advice is to invite death.

Of all the tribes in Gabon the Fang tribe is most feared for its reputation for swift, lethal revenge. Steve could not know that he had just killed a Fang woman. Conditioned by a lifetime of Christian teaching and American law, he immediately pulled the car over to the side of the road and stopped. He, his wife and the missionary got out of the car and ran over to the inert woman to see if they could help. When they saw that she was dead, they carried her body off the road and laid it on the side. They were too stunned to think of their own safety.

By this time the people began milling around the trio. Some began hitting them with their fists and slapping them. A large man kicked the missionary woman from behind. Steve's wife tried to protect her dazed husband from the blows landing on him. With her hand she deflected a punch from his face. Only later did she discover the blow had broken her hand. Several in the group ran to their houses to find machetes and to spread the news.

Steve, his wife and the missionary realized that the crowd was shocked and angered, but they had not yet comprehended that barring a miracle, they had only minutes to live. Instead of seeking refuge in the car, they tried to reason with the crowd. As precious seconds ticked by, someone reached into the truck and removed the keys.

At that moment, a miracle occurred.

The Chief of Police from Libreville was driving to a nearby town when he saw a crowd of twenty or thirty people ahead on the road. In the center, three white foreigners were trying to protect themselves. As he pulled his car to a stop and saw the body of the victim, he understood what had happened. He was in uniform and driving an official car. In a loud voice he began ordering the crowd away from the foreigners. As the mob hesitated, he led the three to their car, ordered them inside and told them to roll up the windows and lock the doors. His quick action saved their lives.

For nearly an hour the stunned trio sat in the stifling car while the police calmed the crowd and took statements from witnesses. Some in the crowd came up to the car and screamed threats and insults at them, but the police managed to protect them from any further harm. Finally, one of the officers retrieved the keys, got in and drove them to the police station. Steve was confined to a room in the barracks. The missionary was allowed to call the Mission director, Clarence Walker, in Libreville.

An hour later Clarence arrived. He asked the police chief if he could stay with Steve while Steve's wife and the missionary who owned the car continued on to Libreville in his car. The police chief agreed. When Clarence saw where Steve was being detained he pointed out to the police chief that the victim's relatives lived only a few kilometers away and that unless a guard was posted outside the door and the outside window someone could easily get into Steve's room. The police chief finally proposed that they all go to a recently built luxury hotel in a town ten kilometers away. Clarence and Steve gratefully accepted. Had the case been left in the hands of the local police Steve would most certainly have been left alone and unprotected during the night. It does not take much imagination to think of what might have happened.

As news of the accident spread, our missionaries and the national Christians responded with a great outpouring of prayer on Steve's behalf. Steve and Clarence remained in the hotel for three days until the police investigation was completed and the paperwork was ready to be forwarded to Libreville. The investigation ab-

solved Steve of any wrongdoing. He was freed
without bail until a judge could hear his case and
determine if he could leave the country. This
was a tremendous answer to prayer.

It can take up to two months to get a judicial
hearing in Gabon, but in less than two weeks
Steve's case came to trial. The judge ruled that
since no crime had been committed, Steve
could leave the country. The Mission was held
responsible to reach a financial settlement with
the family, but since the Mission was covered by
liability insurance, the problem was turned over
to the insurance company for final settlement.

Steve will probably never know why God allowed that fatal accident on the road to Libreville.
Steve's initial reaction was to vow never again to
leave the safety of America. Yet he had to acknowledge that when he was completely helpless
and in the gravest danger he had ever encountered, God had delivered him.

25

Valentine

In typical African fashion I found out from the printed program mailed two months in advance that I was to speak at the upcoming pastors' retreat. The subject was to be: "The Servant of God and Illness." I did not want to go or to speak. I already had too much to do, the road was terrible and my car made ominous noises when it moved. Had I not gone, I would have missed one of the most dramatic experiences of my missionary career.

The retreat was held in Moabi where our earliest missionaries began evangelizing the Bapounou people some forty-five years before. Nearly sixty pastors, evangelists and church workers from most of the provinces in Gabon came to the retreat, along with about ten missionaries. In spite of my initial reluctance, I sensed that God was going to do something special in Moabi.

The French established a colonial military post at Moabi in the early 1900s. In the 1940s Alliance missionaries established their mission two miles away and called it Ileka. People began to settle around the mission. The French colonialists eventually established Moabi as a provincial center, building administrative buildings, schools and a hospital. Over the years, as merchants moved in and built stores, Moabi eclipsed the mission in importance. The people gradually moved away from Ileka, abandoning its large church, its school buildings and its beautiful grounds in favor of the town.

Recognizing the significance of Moabi, however, the missionaries built a new church in the center of town. It was in this church that we were meeting.

I chose to speak to the pastors on how illness can affect the whole man, including his body, his spirit and his soul. I talked at some length about how sin and unresolved guilt can produce both emotional and physical illness. Then, from the point of view of a physician, I began talking about spiritual illnesses. After describing the symptoms and how spirits can sometimes cause them, I told the pastors that in Jesus Christ God had provided them with the power and means to cure spiritual illness. I further explained that physicians, unless they are Christians, do not have this power or knowledge. I challenged the pastors to take the lead in delivering people from spiritual illness and bondage.

I could see that they were excited by what I was saying. It was not new to them but, coming from a medical doctor, it confirmed the Scriptures to them in a practical way. Several times they broke into the discussion with questions.

The most dramatic interruption came when a strange woman walked dazedly into the center of the church and stood in the front, looking at the astonished pastors and missionaries.

Her hair and clothes were a mess, her eyes glazed. Saliva dribbled from the corner of her mouth. It was clear to all of us that the woman was emotionally or spiritually disturbed or both. I suggested that I finish my message later and that the church leaders take charge of the bizarre situation.

The local pastor, Jean Mbadinga, pulled a chair into the center front of the church and, leading the woman to the chair, had her sit down. As she sat mutely and uncomprehendingly, Pastor Mbadinga described to us the situation as he knew it.

The woman's French name was Valentine and she was a new Christian, having accepted the Lord several months before. Prior to her conversion she had been the secret concubine of the leader of another faith. During the ten years of this relationship she had given birth to six of this man's children. Maintaining a public facade of celibacy, he never acknowledged his relationship with her nor with the children he fathered. On several occasions she had tried to leave him, but when he threatened her with eternal damnation, she stayed. In desperation she came to the local Alliance pastor and subsequently met the living Christ. Soon after, she left the man with whom she had been living.

Although she had become a Christian, Valentine was still extremely fearful of this man. To make matters worse, she had no means of supporting her children.

On the first night of the retreat the church leaders showed the first two reels of the *Jesus* film in the center of town. Valentine was among the three or four thousand people who watched the film that night. For some unknown reason, seeing Jesus portrayed in the film threw her into a panic. Late that night she became catatonic, not moving, speaking, seeing or hearing. She lay rigid, her eyes staring. Her children and family rushed her to the local hospital where the French doctor—with whom I was staying—hospitalized and sedated her. He diagnosed her as acutely psychotic.

That same night her family came to Pastor Jean Mbadinga and asked him to come to the hospital to pray for her since the doctor hadn't managed to do much for her. When the pastor saw her, he sensed that she had a spiritual problem. He immediately began praying for her, in Jesus' name, commanding the spirits that were binding her to release her. After an hour of prayer, he noted that she was no longer rigid and could sit up. She seemed able to see, but was not able to hear or speak.

He left instructions with the family to continue to pray during the night. He also told them that if they called in a sorcerer to find out who was cursing her or asked one to make a deal with the spirits, he would not come back to help.

Morning found Valentine sitting on the edge of her bed pointing out the door, indicating that she wanted to go somewhere. They finally decided she was pointing in the direction of the church in the center of town. They led her there, arriving just as I challenged the pastors to treat spiritual disease with spiritual weapons.

Valentine's strange walk from the hospital to the church attracted a crowd of at least fifty family members and curious onlookers. Fortunately, when she entered, they were content to wait outside the church, peering in the open door and windows.

By this time the pastors realized they should do something. The missionaries had some ideas, but wisely held back, wanting the pastors to take the lead and knowing there were those who could. Finally, Moundounga Michel, the dynamic pastor of the Port Gentil Church, stood up.

"Brothers," he said, "this encounter is of the Lord. It is the Lord who timed this woman's arrival with the doctor's message. God has chosen to demonstrate His power among us right now. Let's not disappoint Him!"

Sweeping everyone up in the tide of his faith, he instructed us to form a circle around the dazed woman. Then he asked several of the pastors to pray, commanding the spirits to leave the woman and asking God to deliver her from the bondage of

Satan. As the men commanded and prayed, we lifted our joined hands over Valentine's head.

After ten minutes, Pastor Michel called for silence and ordered Valentine to speak. For the first time she seemed able to hear and understand, but she could not speak. Pastor Michel had us praying together again, commanding the spirit that was preventing her from speaking to release her and commanding all spirits to leave her immediately. After five more minutes, Pastor Michel stopped again to ask her to speak. She complied, but her speech was blurred as though she were drunk. Again we formed a circle of prayer and another pastor commanded the spirits to leave her and prayed for her complete deliverance. Pastor Michel again commanded Valentine to speak the name of Jesus. With tears streaming down her cheeks she easily and freely spoke that name. Pastor Michel asked her to repeat after him that Jesus Christ took on the form of a man when He came to earth and that He is the Lord of all creation. Clearly and joyously she repeated his words.

By now most of us were wiping tears from our eyes. The loud praying and the shouts of praise from inside the church attracted nearly a hundred people, many of them leaning inside the windows to see what was happening.

Valentine recounted how that after seeing the *Jesus* film she had fallen into a dark dungeon where she could neither see nor hear nor speak and how God had led her to come to the church.

At this point, Pastor Michel asked her to pray, thanking Jesus for delivering her from Satan's power and asking for His protection. As she prayed, her voice grew in strength, until everyone both inside and outside the church could hear her thanking and praising God.

By nightfall all of Moabi knew that God had miraculously delivered Valentine. That night when the final reel of the *Jesus* film was shown, over a hundred people prayed to receive Jesus Christ for the first time.

One day some months later, as I finished up my consultations, I felt lead to go talk with a young man I had admitted several days earlier with advanced tuberculosis. After spending months following the sorcerer's advice and wasting a great deal of money, the young man had finally come to the hospital. We immediately started anti-tuberculosis treatment, but he had not eaten for days and slipped into a coma. On this day he finally came out of the coma. I wanted to talk to him while I could.

I sat down next to his bed and carefully explained to him the way of salvation. He asked if he could still be forgiven for his past life, if it was not too late for him to become a child of God. After I assured him that it was not too late and read him the Scriptures promising forgiveness and eternal life, he prayed and accepted Jesus into his heart.

I noticed someone listening just outside the door, but by the time I left the room the person had gone. As I walked away from the building an attractive, middle-aged woman called to me.

"Do you remember me, doctor?" she asked. With some embarrassment I confessed that I did not.

"I'm the woman the pastors prayed for at Moabi!" I could not hide my astonishment. She explained that she was renting one of our hospital rooms while following treatment for a urinary infection.

"I was listening by the door while you were talking to the young man about Jesus. I've been talking to him about Jesus, too, and told him how Jesus delivered me from the power of the spirits." Her face glowed with joy as she spoke.

As I walked up the path to my home, I marveled at God's ways and at my own lack of faith. God had used me in a small way in Moabi and now the fruit of that obedience had touched a young man dying of tuberculosis in my hospital. He, too, would live forever.

26

Casualties of the Warfare

The young woman writhing in pain on the examining table held her hand over her left ear. She was fifteen years old and her older sister had accompanied her to the hospital. I managed to get her to sit still long enough to examine the outside of her ear and then to look inside with an otoscope. It looked perfectly normal.

She was running a fever of about 102 degrees, but she had no other physical findings. Baffled, I treated her symptoms with strong medication both for pain and malaria.

The next day her fever was gone but the pain in her ear was worse. I examined her again. Everything appeared to be normal. She denied any history of trauma to her face, head or ear and was able to open her mouth and chew without difficulty. Because she was in agony from the pain, and since the oral pain medication had not helped, I gave her an injection of morphine. During the night she was in so much pain that I increased the dose and combined it with a tranquilizer. Even that did not help.

On morning rounds I suggested to her that God could heal her and that if she was willing, we would pray for her. She preferred instead to return to her village to consult the sorcerer. Somewhat taken aback, I asked how she thought that would help. She was in too much pain to offer much of an explanation, but her sister said something to the effect that her spirit had left her body "in vampire." It sounded so bizarre that I decided to ask Pastor Philippe about it.

Pastor Philippe did not seem surprised. He explained that she was from the Mitsogo tribe. The Mitsogo believe that every person has a friendly spirit who inhabits them in addition to their own. If this spirit becomes offended by something its owner does or becomes seriously ill or is injured in an accident, the spirit may leave. When it wanders around outside of the owner's body, the Mitsogo say that it is "in vampire." When the spirit leaves, the person it has left can experience any number of unpleasant symptoms.

A spirit "in vampire" is a matter of grave concern to everyone in the village because when a friendly spirit decides to leave its host, it becomes unfriendly. It can cause illnesses, accidents, family fights and even death in the community. The only solution is to call in the sorcerer to placate the spirit and call it back into the person it left.

When the people in the girl's community learned that I was not able to help her, they decided that the problem was spiritual. Unknown to me, they had ordered her to return to the village or face serious consequences. The pastor had counseled her against having anything more to do with the spirits and had offered to help her escape from the spirit that was torturing her. She refused.

He could see that I was skeptical, so he suggested that since the girl was determined to go to the sorcerer that I take her to the village and talk to the sorcerer myself. He felt I needed to understand that the power of the spirits was not imagined or just superstition. It was real.

The pastor accompanied me as I drove the girl the thirty kilometers to her village. During the trip she cried and held her head in her hands. Because of continuous pain, she had not been able to eat for three days and she had lost about five pounds.

The village elders were relieved to see her, and as she got out of the car they hustled her over to the sorcerer's house. The pastor asked a bystander to tell the sorcerer that I wanted to see him. A few minutes later he emerged from the house. He looked very ordinary and was dressed in simple clothes. There was nothing to distinguish him from any other man in the village.

He greeted me with a friendly handshake and to my chagrin thanked me for bringing the girl back to him. I asked him to explain what he thought the problem was. His explanation was almost identical to the pastor's. He said that he planned to call the wandering spirit back into the girl that same evening. He agreed to send her back to me the next day so I could see for myself that she was well. It disturbed me that he had not the slightest doubt that his treatment would result in a cure. The pastor seemed amused at my continued skepticism.

"You will learn, doctor," he said gently, "that evil spirits can perform miracles, too."

The next afternoon the girl appeared at the hospital, having walked all morning. She was smiling and showed no signs of illness. She related that during the ceremony she had felt the spirit come back into her body. The pain in her ear immediately ceased.

A great sadness filled me as I watched her walk away. Unwilling to place her faith in Christ, she had received a cure. Unfortunately, it was at the price of her soul.

Marie was fifteen years old and unmarried when she became pregnant. This is not unusual, since most girls in Gabon get pregnant at a young age before marrying. Sterility due to venereal disease is such a serious problem in Gabon that a young girl must prove she can have children before a man will marry her. In proving herself, she usually contracts one or more venereal diseases and all too often ends up unable to conceive. This was not Marie's concern, however.

After a long and very difficult labor at a nearby government hospital, Marie gave birth to a normal

baby. Two days later, she became totally blind.
The family brought her to our hospital the next
day, expressing hope that I would be able to cure
her. I had never seen a similar case, and I was unable to find out anything about it in our limited li-
brary.

Her neurological and eye examinations appeared completely normal, except, of course,
that she couldn't see anything. Since I thought
there was a possibility the problem was temporary, I encouraged the family to pray and trust
God to heal her. In any case, not wanting to
make things worse, and not knowing what to do
anyway, I thought it best to wait and see.

Because they considered praying and waiting
equivalent to doing nothing, Marie's parents
were understandably unhappy with my sugges-
tion. They decided to take Marie to the sorcerer.

The witch doctor will always remain important in African life because of his ability to enlist
the powers and help those who come to him for
aid. The Gabonese believe that there are good
spirits and evil spirits, but even the good spirits
are not totally good, since they can cause harm
when angered. The sorcerer believes that he can
manipulate the spirits to serve his or her clients'
purposes. The spirits reveal secrets to him, punish those he wishes to harm through illness or
accident, bring healing from spirit-initiated illness, kill others and protect his clients.

The Bible teaches that the world is filled not
only with plant, animal and human life but also

with spiritual beings. These spiritual beings are invisible to us and are in continual conflict. The evil spirits seek to enslave and destroy humans. They succeed through deception, convincing those who contact them that they are really good, useful and willing to offer their services with no obligation. What these spirits do not reveal is that their real intent is to inhabit humans and thereby control them. The ultimate victory for these shadowy beings is the death of their host.

The Bible also teaches that these deceiving spirits are powerful and numerous on the earth. Their chief is Satan himself. They are not, however, unopposed. Their greatest enemy is the Being who created them and Who created the universe. They rebelled against their Creator and He threw them out of heaven and down to the earth. That same eternal Being visited the earth He had created in a human body. His name is Jesus Christ. The Bible calls His spiritual assistants and servants angels. They are good and powerful spirits who fight against Satan and his evil spirits. It is the name of Jesus and the power that name represents that the evil spirits of the world fear more than anything else in the universe.

I did not hear anything more about Marie for a month. Then one day she appeared. Her eyesight had returned and her family wanted me to know that it was the sorcerer who had cured her. It is possible that the spirits were responsible for Marie's restored sight, but it could also have been the spontaneous resolution of a temporary medical problem. Nevertheless, it was useless to claim that it was anything other than a spiritual healing. The sorcerer received great credit for this supposed miracle.

The last time I saw Marie I was impressed by her sadness. Instead of joy at seeing and enjoying her baby, she was listless and disinterested in life. It seemed that in asking the spirits to help her she had enslaved herself to them in ways that she would not easily escape.

Deep in the jungle, a young Christian named Fidele opposed the spirits and paid for it dearly. He had been a Christian for about five years and he and his young wife felt God calling them into the ministry. He was appointed to lead a small band of Christians in his home village of Lepoye.

Fidele and his wife had three small children and were devoted to each other. They both came from first-generation Christian families that were still struggling to free themselves from centuries of pagan tradition.

Fidele's knowledge of the Bible was very limited, but because he had experienced its power in his own life, he could explain it clearly and enthusiastically. He knew absolutely nothing, however, about spiritual warfare.

The district pastor, under whose tutelage Fidele was being taught, had great respect for the spirits. He understood that immorality, dishonesty, hatred or other sins could expose people to their power. But he had no knowledge of the principles of spiritual warfare except for prayer.

Fidele had been pastoring the church in Lepoye for about two years when one day his wife noticed a change in his behavior. One week later he began hallucinating and talking to himself. Finally he became so violent and irrational that she and the children fled the house and found refuge in a neighboring Christian's home. The people of the church were frightened and bewildered. If the spirits could drive their young pastor out of his mind, what could happen to them? They prayed for God to deliver Fidele.

In most Gabonese communities there are certain sorcerers who specialize in treating people with bizarre or aberrant behavior. They are not considered ordinary witch doctors, although most of them invoke the spirits as part of their treatment with psychoactive herbal preparations.

There was no real insanity specialist in Lepoye, so the family locked Fidele in a mud brick, windowless room and sent word for the witch doctor from a neighboring village to come. Several crude attempts were made to treat him, but he only got worse. Fidele tried to dig himself out of the room. To keep him from doing more damage or from escaping into the forest, the family dragged in a tree trunk and tied his hands around it.

Dr. Doug Hall, one of our missionary doctors, visited the village one day and found Fidele tied to the log and in appalling condition. The stench of his body, his unkempt appearance and his bizarre behavior made him seem more animal than man. Dr. Hall asked the family's permission to take Fidele to the hospital, but they refused.

When the district pastor learned of Fidele's loss of reason he did not know what to do. He finally decided to just let Fidele's family take care of him. It was common knowledge that years before Fidele had temporarily lost his sanity. Had Fidele compromised himself by a secret sin? Had he fallen into immorality? Or was this a simple case of mental instability? The pastor concluded that it was probably mental illness. The implications and outworkings of that decision were tragic.

The herbal specialist began treatment and moved Fidele to his village, which was also the district pastor's village and the community where Fidele's wife now lived with her parents. By this time Fidele was becoming cooperative and able to care for his bodily needs. He saw the specialist every day and was given various herbal concoctions that made him sleep long hours.

Over the protests of Fidele's wife, her family began divorce proceedings. This meant returning the dowry that Fidele had paid them to marry her. Fidele's family agreed that divorce was in their best interest, too, especially since they would benefit materially at a time when they needed cash to pay the specialist. Although both families were supposed to be Christians and although everyone in the church knew what was happening, the divorce proceedings quietly went forward. The church made no effort to intervene in the tragedy that was unfolding before them.

With the passage of time Fidele began to emerge from his nightmare. He pled to be reunited with his wife and children, but his request fell on deaf ears. It is still possible, assuming that neither chooses new partners in the meantime, that Fidele and his wife might find each other again. But it is unlikely, because when a spiritual ambush came against one of God's servants, the church bowed to tradition and was left standing powerless and mute on the sidelines. A promising shepherd and his family were destroyed in the process.

Will either Fidele or his wife ever again serve Christ with the same zeal that characterized their early days in Lepoye? I don't know. But, thank God, there is no life from whose ashes God cannot again grow something beautiful.

27

Into the Night

C hristian appeared at the hospital one day complaining of terrible pain just about everywhere. He was a muscular, healthy-looking twenty-year-old, but he moaned and groaned so effectively during his examination that I finally admitted him to the hospital. During the following week he never ran a fever and seemed remarkably active for someone with such severe symptoms. When after two weeks of various creative medical therapies we proposed to discharge him, he came up with a new list of symptoms. We began to suspect he was a shirker.

Finally one day we needed his bed for someone who was very ill, so we discharged him and told him to come back to the outpatient clinic whenever he needed treatment. He nearly cried, begging to be allowed to stay anywhere on the hospital grounds. For the first time I realized that he was afraid to leave. *But why?* I wondered to myself. We finally decided to let him stay in an empty storage room.

During the following weeks we saw Christian often in church services and around the hospital. The chaplain talked with him for many hours, and Christian told him that he had come to the hospital to escape spirits that were haunting him. For years, he said, spirits had talked to him at night, telling him to do certain things. He had tried to ignore them, but they became increasingly insistent and finally began to threaten him. When someone told him that our hospital was a place where God was, he decided to come. The moment he stepped onto the hospital grounds the spirits became subdued.

When the chaplain related this to me I concluded that Christian was probably a budding schizophrenic. Still, I wondered. A week later Christian prayed to receive Christ as his Savior.

Christian was very intelligent and told us that he had completed two years at the university in Libreville. While a student, he consulted several sorcerers to enhance his ability to learn. This is not unusual in Gabon. The sorcerer also sold him a sacred object called a fetish to give him special intelligence, a sort of good luck charm.

Soon afterward he began hearing voices at night, but he never associated the voices with the fetish. In fact, he went back to the sorcerer to try to obtain protection and relief from the voices, which he concluded were spirits. Additional fetishes did not help and the problem progressed to where he could not sleep at night. He finally had to drop out of school. Until coming to our hospital he had been unable to find relief.

The hospital needed a new trash pit, so we hired Christian for the job. He worked so well that we gave him another job to do. When there was no more work at the hospital, I hired him to care for the lawns around the mission houses.

Christian was a member of the Bapounou tribe. Rev. Raymond Cook, one of the first to preach the gospel to the Bapounou in the early '40s, was back at Bongolo for one year on special assignment. Pastor Philippe asked Rev. Cook to disciple Christian.

Every day after work Christian went to Ray Cook's office for an hour of Bible study, discussion and prayer. He showed a remarkable ability to understand the Word of God and his spiritual growth was exciting to watch. Three months after his conversion, Christian was ready to be baptized as a public indication of his belief in Christ.

On several occasions Ray Cook and I asked Christian about his family, but he was curiously reluctant to talk about them. When pressed, he explained that his parents had died and his closest living relative was an uncle. He was terrified of this uncle and believed that it was his uncle who had sent the spirits to torment him at the university.

Before baptism, Christian assured the pastor that he had destroyed all his fetishes. Nevertheless, he did not feel that his newfound faith was strong enough to stand against his uncle's personality and spiritual powers. Although all of us felt he should declare his new faith in Christ to his family before he was baptized, he convinced us that he should wait until later before reestablishing contact with his uncle. He was baptized in the Louetsi River on Christmas day.

Christian was one of the most exuberant Christians I've ever known. From the day of his conversion, all he wanted to do was talk or sing about Christ and about his deliverance from the spirits. You could hear his strong, baritone voice singing songs of praise above the roar of the lawn mower as he mowed the grass. Except for his fear of his uncle, he gave no evidence of mental or emotional imbalance. When asked why he was so happy, he would smile and say, "Because Jesus set me free!" To this day I do not doubt that his conversion was genuine.

A year later Christian announced that he wanted to become a pastor. This generated considerable discussion among the pastors and missionaries. Some felt it was too soon after his conversion, others wondered about his almost complete isolation from his family. But none doubted his love for the Lord or his sincerity in following Christ. He argued convincingly that his decision to follow Christ was what separated him from his family.

A special bond developed between Ray Cook and Christian, and Ray's counsel and encouragement seemed to influence him the most. Ray and the church leaders decided that if Christian wanted to go to Bible school, he would have to reestablish contact with his family and inform them of his decision.

It was almost a month before Christian felt ready to go. During this time many of us counseled him and prayed with him. Although he expressed fear that his uncle might somehow strip him of his faith in Christ, he refused to let anyone accompany him.

He was gone for about two weeks and during that time we prayed for him often. When he returned we welcomed him warmly and asked him what happened. His answers were disturbingly vague. Apparently, his family had accepted his decision to follow Christ. His uncle had not been a problem.

I felt that for some reason Christian was hiding something from us, but in response to my questioning, he assured me that he had told us everything. Nevertheless, I wondered if he had really visited his family. Something did not ring true. Several weeks later he was accepted as a first-year student at the Bible school.

It was two months before I heard from him again. He wrote in a letter that although his studies were progressing well, he was again experiencing abdominal pain. There was something else in this letter that disturbed me—he wanted me to pray that he would resist. My question was, "Resist what?"

About this same time his fellow students at the school noticed that Christian was eating strangely.

First he stopped eating meat. For a Bible school student, that was not unreasonable since meat was so expensive. But then he stopped eating anything prepared from palm nuts. Since palm oil is about the only cooking oil available in the interior, this posed a real problem.

He began to lose weight and became increasingly eccentric. He started fasting, first one meal a day, then one day a week, then several days a week. At night he sang aloud for hours. The other students did not recognize any of the songs.

Christian began taking long walks in the forest. At first he went for an hour or two, but then he disappeared for entire afternoons. Finally, he stayed out all night.

The Gabonese are afraid to be out alone at night because they believe that the night belongs to the spirits. Even on hot, humid nights the Gabonese close up every window and door in the house. It does not matter if the windows are screened or if the family is sleeping under a mosquito net. The windows must be closed. If asked, they will tell you that they do it to keep out thieves, but even if the window has security bars, they will be uneasy until it is shuttered. When Christian stayed out in the forest all night, his classmates were horrified. It could only mean that he wanted to be there. To them that meant that he was either mad or consorting with the spirits.

When he returned to school the next morning, Pastor Moukingui, the dean of students, went to talk to him. Christian said he had been talking with an angel. It was the angel that had told him to stop eating the products of the palm tree and all meat. It was the angel that taught him the songs he sang at night. And it was the angel who led him into the forest and communed with him all night.

Pastor Moukingui asked Christian to describe the angel. It was a being of great beauty, Christian said, very bright and glowing, like a white-hot coal. He was certain that the angel was sent by God to help him. Pastor Moukingui was not able to convince him otherwise.

On a hunch, Pastor Moukingui asked Christian if he had kept any of the fetishes from his pagan life. He would not admit to having a fetish, and he refused to break off his relationship with the angel.

The school directors decided to bring Christian back to Bongolo. Perhaps those who had led him to Christ would be able to counsel him. Christian seemed to think this was a good idea.

I was in my office seeing patients when Pastor Moukingui arrived. After the customary greetings and friendly banter, we got down to the subject of Christian. Moukingui recounted everything that had happened at the school. We prayed together and decided finally that the local pastors should first talk with Christian. Ray Cook had returned to the States, but I promised to see Christian that evening.

The meeting between Christian and the pastors did not go well. Christian was evasive and distracted. He was like a closed book, and no-body could pry the covers open. The pastors finally told him that I wanted to see him around 7 p.m. He agreed to come if I was alone.

At 8 o'clock he appeared suddenly on my front porch. I greeted him like an old friend and we sat down. He asked me to turn out the porch light and somewhat reluctantly I did. I asked him how he was doing.

For about five minutes he said nothing. As we sat there in absolute silence, I prayed for wisdom and discernment, wondering if he was psychotic or spiritually troubled. Finally he spoke.

"I have learned many wonderful things since I left here."

"In the Bible, you mean?" I asked, trying to get the conversation going.

"Well, in the Bible, but from other places as well."

"What other places?" I asked.

"From an angel of God," he replied, starting to warm up.

"What's the angel like?"

"He is very beautiful and very wise. He glows like a white light."

"What does he tell you?" I persisted.

"If I will be obedient to God, he will do miracles through me," Christian replied.

"How do you know the angel is from God?" I wondered aloud.

"Believe me," Christian answered forcefully, "I know! I can tell the difference between an evil spirit and an angel of God!"

"How?"

"By what he says. He says that the Bible is true and that I am on the right path. God has sent him to lead me on that path."

"What does he say about Jesus?" I asked.

"He says he is Jesus' messenger and spokesman," he explained.

"Is it true that you have not destroyed all your old fetishes?" I queried. His friendly mood changed immediately.

"Who told you that I have kept fetishes?" There was anger in his voice now and I began to sense the presence of great evil.

"Do you still have your old fetishes?" I probed as gently as I could. "If you have kept even one, it gives Satan the right to oppress you." A minute of heavy silence passed.

"The angel told me to keep them, so I did."

"But Christian, the Bible says that Christians must have nothing to do with things that belong to Satan. Why would an angel of God contradict God?"

"It is an angel of God, I tell you!" he almost shouted, leaning forward in his chair. "Do you want to see him for yourself?" A feeling of apprehension passed over me. There was indeed something terribly evil with us on that porch. I could feel the hair stand up on the back of my neck. My arms were covered with goosebumps.

"I don't need to see him to know that he does not come from God and that he is deluding you, Christian. An angel of God would never permit you to keep a fetish! He is taking you off to hell! Christian, if you want to follow Jesus, you must renounce this evil angel. Otherwise he will have you in his power forever!"

With that, Christian leaped to his feet and stood over me, his hands clenching and unclenching, his breathing heavy. I sat motionless, praying for God to protect me. After a long minute he relaxed and leaned against the porch wall. He would not look at me, and he said nothing.

"Christian," I said gently, "you are being deceived by an angel of light. That is Satan's oldest tactic. It's what he did in the garden of Eden when the world began. He may look like an angel of God, but he is evil, and when he has finished with you he will destroy you. I beg you, Christian, let me help you get free of this thing."

Without another word he spun on his heel and walked off the porch into the night. His bare feet on the lawn made his departure noiseless and the black night seemed to swallow him whole. I prayed silently for him, then got up and went into the house.

The next morning I told Moukingui and the Bongolo pastors what had happened. During the day someone saw him enter his room and emerge a few minutes later with his machete and a small shoulder bag. Without saying a word to anyone he walked into the forest.

We never saw Christian or heard from him again. We eventually found his uncle. He told us that he had not seen Christian since he had gone to the university in Libreville two years before. The family had thought that Christian was dead. My suspicions that Christian had never visited his uncle were true.

Christian's whereabouts remain a mystery. Perhaps he wandered into the nearby Republic of Congo. Perhaps he is among Libreville's masses. Perhaps he is dead.

The reasons behind his strange behavior, however, are not a mystery. In consulting a sorcerer and buying his sacred object and charms, Christian acquiesced to evil spiritual beings. When he came into the light of Jesus Christ he was temporarily free of their harassments—until he decided to keep several of the fetishes as a safety net. In making that decision, he turned back into the night of Satan's power and bondage. His final capitulation occurred when he allowed himself to be seduced by an evil angel of beauty and light who appeared to him and promised him success and power. Such is the deceptive power of Satan. Only prayer and the overcoming power of God can deliver him from Satan's grasp now.

28

Makaya

The little man sitting in front of me was upset, and the dusty fan wobbling in the corner did little to move the sticky air in my office. I waited for Makaya to decide whether or not he was going to follow my advice to remain in the hospital until we got his irregular heartbeat controlled.

"Doctor," he finally managed, "I did not come all the way from Tchibanga today prepared to stay. The car that brought my wife and me for this checkup is waiting across the river. We didn't bring our things to stay. We didn't come with any money to pay for the hospital bill or even to buy food to eat while we're here."

"Makaya," I said firmly, "your heart has a very dangerous rhythm. It could stop suddenly while you're on your way home." I could picture him bouncing around in the back of an open pickup truck for three hours over the rough dirt roads. "You must stay here until your heart is regulated."

He sighed heavily. "Very well, I'll stay. But if I'm to eat, I'll need some money. Will you lend me $75?"

My mind grappled with his question. Seventy-five dollars? Loan one of my patients $75? If I made it a habit, I'd soon be a pauper. Besides, I didn't have $75 to spare! Or did I? Someone was interfering with my thoughts and disturbing words appeared in my mind's eye: "Give to the one who asks you and do not turn away from the one who wants to borrow from you." I recognized them as Jesus' words from the Sermon on the Mount. I knew that I had received a direct command. I paused to compose a smile, and although I had serious misgivings, I told Makaya that I would give him the money in the morning. Relief and gratitude spread across his face.

I instructed a nurse to find a bed for Makaya in one of our few private rooms. The next morning when I walked into his room, I was shocked at what I saw. Makaya had ended up in a room with an upper-class female patient, Brigitte, who was still recovering from major surgery! I had promised her that she and her daughter would have the room to themselves and now we had put a man in her room! I could not believe the nurses had been so insensitive and not informed me of the problem. The daughter had given up the second bed in the room and was sleeping with her mother. Makaya and his wife had the other bed. I apologized profusely to both of them for the embarrassing situation and immediately set out to find another bed and another room for Makaya. I searched in vain all over the hospital. When I explained the situation to Brigitte, she smiled and shrugged. "Perhaps," she said, "the Lord wants it this way." Her remark prompted a surprised look from both Makaya and me.

Makaya had retired from the civil service in Tchibanga several years before. I didn't know it at the time, but for years missionaries working in Tchibanga had tried to talk to him about the Lord. His job was delivering messages between different government officials in town. He was always in a hurry running here or there and didn't care to stop to hear someone talk about the Lord. Anyway, as a devout Catholic, he was not interested in the Protestant religion. From my brief contact with him, I knew that Makaya did not know God.

Brigitte, on the other hand, was a faithful believer. She had come over 800 kilometers from eastern Gabon to have surgery at our hospital. Our staff was impressed by her quiet and gentle spirit.

Several days later I made rounds again and when I came into Makaya and Brigitte's room it was clear that the two families had become friends. I asked if either of them would like to move to another room, since another bed was now available. Much to my surprise, they declined. With a faint smile, Brigitte explained that both Makaya and his wife had prayed with the hospital chaplain the night before to receive Christ as their Lord and Savior. Now that they had found the Lord she wanted to take every opportunity to teach them to follow Him.

Several days later, both Brigitte and Makaya were discharged from the hospital. Makaya had an appointment to return for a checkup in two months. Before the time arrived, I left with my family on a vacation to the coast. The trip took us through Tchibanga. We stopped at the church to deliver some books to the local pastor. He seemed very happy to see us. "How are things going?" I asked.

"Well," he said, his face beaming, "the church is overflowing every Sunday. We don't have enough room for all the people who are coming to the Lord and coming to church!" This was wonderful news indeed. "You know," he added thoughtfully, "there's a fellow who's attending the church now who found the Lord in your hospital. He and his wife faithfully come to every meeting, and they have brought many others into the church, too."

"Is his name Makaya?" I wondered.

"Why, yes!" he exclaimed, slapping his hands together. "That's him! What a blessing he has been to me and to this church!"

Makaya turned up as scheduled for his checkup. His heart was ticking along smoothly, and he thanked me and praised the Lord for restoring his health. Then he took out $75 and handed it to me. Somewhat confused, I explained to him that he should pay his bill at the cashier's office. A look of amusement crossed his face.

"Doctor, I'm repaying you the money you loaned me. Don't you remember?" Embarrassed at my lapse of memory, I laughed and took the bills. He became serious as he stood up to leave.

"You know, doctor, you're one of the reasons I found Jesus. When you loaned me that money, I knew that God was in this place and that you loved God. You hardly knew me, and you had no way of getting the money back if I didn't bring it. When Brigitte began talking to me about Jesus, I had already decided I wanted to follow Him." I could barely choke out a goodbye as he left. It had never entered my mind that by loaning a stranger $75 I would prepare his heart to meet Christ.

Makaya was won to Christ because of sacrifice—not just my sacrifice and not just Brigitte's sacrifice, but the sacrifice of many of God's people. God's people pay for me and my family to live and work in Gabon. God's people pray that what we do will win people to Christ. God's people collect and send medicine and needed supplies to the hospital. All over the world the sacrifices of God's people are winning people like Makaya to Christ.

29

The Bridge to Bongolo

The battered pickup with its load of dusty passengers eased over the crest of the hill and slowed to a stop where the road disappeared into the river. Reluctantly legs and bodies were swung over the side of the truck along with bags, bundles, and baskets of belongings. One woman, however, remained motionless in the back of the truck until her husband lowered the tailgate and helped her get down. People on the riverbank noticed that her face was pinched and thin, but her abdomen was enormous. Yet she didn't look pregnant.

The woman's husband half-carried her to the side of the road, lowering her to the ground where once again she lay motionless on her side, exhausted by the effort. The young husband looked at the river and the reappearing road on the far side. "How much farther to the hospital?" he asked hesitantly. The onlookers assured him it was not far once he got across the river. He would, however, have to leave his wife on the other side and walk the kilometer to the hospital to get help.

As the people on the shore watched, a man pulled the 30-foot dugout canoe across the river toward them. They climbed in. With considerable difficulty the woman also got in. Several sympathetic bystanders helped load the couple's baggage into the canoe. When everyone was settled, the crosser pulled the canoe back to the other side and brought it alongside a small pontoon ferry resting in the water. The passengers clambered out of the canoe, walked across the ferry and stepped ashore. Several young men helped the sick woman's husband carry her to the bank.

I was getting medicines and supplies together for a trip to the dispensaries the next morning. I had been in the operating room from 8 until 2 o'clock in the afternoon, and after a half-hour lunch break, found myself counting pills in the airless pharmacy. As I grumbled to myself, a young man walked hesitantly to the door and waited for me to acknowledge his presence. Barely managing to suppress my irritation, I greeted the young man without looking up so he'd appreciate how busy I was.

"My wife," he said in broken French, "my wife is at the river. She is very sick. We came all the way from Eteke today." Eteke had once been a gold mining town. The road through the mountainous rain forest had been well-maintained and controlled to prevent theft. But the gold had run out or had become too expensive to mine, the highway had been neglected and now few cars made the trip. Just the year before, two people had died horribly in Eteke from strangulated hernias because there had been no way to get them out. This couple had been lucky. They had had to wait only five days.

With a sigh I closed up the pharmacy and drove with the young man down to the river. His wife was leaning weakly against the dirt bank and I felt a twinge of guilt. She sat with her legs straight out in front. The thin hands holding her abdomen rose and fell with her rapid breathing. I greeted her in her own language, but she was too weary to even notice. We lifted her onto the back seat of the car, and although the truck bounced on the rough road, she made no sound.

At the hospital I learned that their French names were Veronica and Pascal. After examining her, I determined that she had an intestinal obstruction that had developed at least five days earlier. Having vomited frequently for five days, she was so dehydrated and weak I was afraid she might die on the operating table.

Her blood count showed that she was severely anemic. Her husband's blood didn't match hers, nor did that of any of the hospital staff. Since there are no blood banks in south Gabon, we had no blood to give her. After rehydrating her with intravenous fluids and starting her on antibiotics, I called in the operating team and took her to surgery. I gave her a spinal anesthetic and the team prayed for wisdom for what had to be done. We also prayed that Jesus Christ would reveal Himself to Veronica and her husband as we cared for her and that they would eventually choose to follow Him.

It was a short prayer. When it was over, the student nurse monitoring the blood pressure announced that Veronica's pressure was too low to measure. Over the next two hours, in the face of shock and intraoperative blood loss, we fought to keep her alive. Without blood we could give her only intravenous salt solutions to maintain her blood pressure. In her abdomen we discovered a bizarre complication of severe pelvic infection, which had caused half of her large intestine to turn black with gangrene. I removed the dead intestine and gave her a temporary colostomy.

By the end of the operation her blood was about the consistency and color of cherry Kool-Aid, but she was alive and conscious. I gave her husband the basin containing the piece of intestine, told him where we kept the shovel and asked him to bury the specimen out behind the hospital. His eyes widened, but he did as I asked. After all, it was a normal request.

Veronica had a difficult night, but by morning her blood pressure was stable and she felt better. I showed her and her husband the colostomy when I changed the dressings. They were shocked at what I had done and indicated by their reaction that death might have been preferable. After several days, when we ran out of colostomy sacks, brutal reality intervened and Veronica was forced to take an active role in its care.

As the days passed and Veronica's strength returned, she and Pascal began to respond ever so slowly to the hospital staff's kindness. Two weeks after surgery Veronica smiled for the first time after I greeted her in her own language. I hoped it was not because I had pronounced the words so oddly!

A month later I reoperated on Veronica, removing her colostomy and reconnecting her intestines. She made a complete and rapid recovery.

Since the couple understood very little French, our Mitsogo-speaking staff talked to them about the way of salvation in Jesus Christ. I do not know if either of them will ever turn from spirit worship to follow Christ, but Veronica is alive and if they choose, they have the opportunity to live forever.

There was no bridge at Bongolo for Veronica and her husband to come to the hospital. There is still no bridge at Bongolo either for cars or pedestrians to cross—only a ferry. Perhaps some day there will be a pedestrian bridge, and one can dream that someday there will be a bridge for cars.

Nevertheless, in 1977 I crossed a bridge at Bongolo. That bridge brought me over a wide and incomprehensible chasm. It brought me to a people I did not know and did not love. It carried me somewhat unwillingly out of my past in Asia and led me to what I perceived to be the darkest continent of all: Africa. It drew me out of a world of enormous wealth and astonishing technology to a world of dirt and poverty, where everything runs down and nothing seems to work. It pulled me from the arms of my family and took me to a place in which I had no interest. It was a bridge built of God's love and grace and of my transient loss and pain. Others walking by faith and in obedience to God had crossed the bridge before me. Although it is invisible, it is the most important bridge to Bongolo.

Note: Since the first printing of this book, the bridge at the Bongolo hospital is done and in service. Praise God!

30

If You Could Only See . . .

Paul Carlson, a missionary doctor martyred in Zaire in 1964 once told an American colleague over lunch, "If you could only see, you wouldn't be able to swallow your sandwich."

Jesus saw and He cared. The Bible tells us that He "went through all the towns and villages, teaching in their synagogues, preaching the good news of the kingdom and healing every disease and sickness" (Matthew 9:35). And in verse 36 of the same chapter we note this astonishing observation: "When he saw the crowds, he had compassion on them." For Jesus, seeing resulted in compassion. On another occasion, alluding to people needing salvation, He said, "I tell you, open your eyes and look at the fields! They are ripe for harvest."

The world is filled with people who are suffering and whose souls after death are doomed to unspeakable, endless horror. Do we see them? Do we even know they are there?

One tropical night in Gabon, a young woman, already in labor, walked two kilometers in the dark to get to the Lebamba hospital. During the night she delivered a healthy baby, but the midwife noticed that the young mother was hemorrhaging more than usual. All efforts to stop the bleeding were unsuccessful, and since the French doctor was away, it was obvious that the girl would have to go to Bongolo. She ordered the family to find the hospital driver.

An hour later the party was on its way in the back of an open pickup truck. When they arrived at the Louetsi River, their hearts sank: both the ferry and the canoe were on the opposite shore. None of them had the courage to swim the swift river at night and the driver was too old to pull himself across hand over hand on the steel cable that spanned the river. As they waited the young woman continued to bleed. The family shouted and finally screamed in the hope that someone—anyone—would hear and come to their aid. But no one heard their cries. None of us knew that they were there.

Early in the morning several people from the village went down to the river to get water. They were surprised to find a truck parked on the opposite shore. When they realized there was a medical emergency, one of them brought the ferry over to the waiting group. The weary driver drove onto the ferry with the now-unconscious woman and crossed the river.

Our medical team sprang into action, but by then it was too late. After a few hours, despite our best efforts, the young woman died of irreversible shock.

It was one of the thousand tragedies that occur every day in what we glibly call the Third World, or for the desperately poor, the Fourth World.

Compared to the nations of the Third and Fourth World, Christians living in North America and Europe have enormous resources. The key to sharing those resources is in looking, in seeing those who wait in poverty and spiritual darkness. Will we lift up our eyes and look beyond our own needs and plans for self-fulfillment? Will we look at people who are outside our families? Will we open our eyes and see what God sees?

It is easier not to look. With our eyes closed we can sleep peacefully, content that the world is improving. If we are careful, we will never be touched by compassion for the poor and the lost. We will not even be aware of them. And, of course, when they die, we will feel no loss.

"Jesus had compassion on them." There is a subtle danger in the Church—the danger that we will use medical, relief or development programs only as a vehicle to win souls to Christ. Such programs can become a mere means, enabling us to reach what we think is really important: souls. While it is true that the body is temporary and souls live forever, there is a coldness to this line of reasoning that chills my heart. The motivation is not love of flesh-and-bone people, but of disembodied people. It moves evangelism into a realm where physical suffering, as long as it is not our own, is relatively unimportant.

I do not believe that Jesus healed people simply as a means to win souls. He hated the disease, deformity, suffering and death that sin brought into the world. So should we. He healed and helped people because He loved them and felt compassion for them. So should we.

I do not mean to say that the Church is responsible to care for all the world's sick or feed all the world's hungry or insure the health and income of all the world's poor. Although there were no doubt thousands of sick children and adults in Palestine, Jesus did not organize a nationwide Primary Health Care Program. Even though on two occasions He miraculously produced food to feed thousands of hungry people, He did not devote His life to feeding the hungry and developing Palestine's agricultural resources. Jesus expressed His love by responding to a person's particular need—spiritual, emotional, physical or all three.

The mission of the Church is to go into all the world and proclaim the gospel, making disciples in the process. But as the Church goes, it needs to follow Christ's model. It needs to accurately represent the Christ who walked the roads of Palestine.

Jesus' point in the story of the Good Samaritan (Luke 10:25-37) is that we are to respond to human need as we encounter it. It is God, after all, who is sovereign over our daily lives. While we are protesting that we can't possibly feed all the poor, God places one beggar in our path. While we are crying that we cannot provide health care for all of Africa, God brings home to an African church its need to do something about the children and adults dying every year in its shadow. As we stop and help those who are lying in our pathway, we demonstrate that we, the disciples of Jesus Christ, love more than souls—we love people.

Some are saying that the day of missionary medicine is nearly over. That may be true in more developed parts of the world, but it will be a long time before it is true in Africa. I am convinced that many significant opportunities are available to missionary medical personnel if we will rise to meet the challenge.

As servants of God, our model is Jesus Christ. The key to any Christian program is not the program itself—it is the individuals who serve. They must love Jesus Christ supremely. They must be led by God's Spirit. They must love the people they are serving more than they love their programs. Above all, they must love the people they are helping more than they love themselves. They must be able to walk in the shoes of those they serve, weep when they weep, rejoice when they rejoice.

As a Christian physician I want my patients to live forever. I also want them to be healthy physically and emotionally. Such a motivation comes straight from the heart of God. The Gabonese must see the Christ who lives in me and the God who sent me to them. The patients at the Bongolo Evangelical Hospital must understand that the peace they feel there comes because of God's power over the dark and malevolent spirits that so relentlessly pursue all who live in darkness.

Also by David Thompson:

Beyond the Mist:
The Story of Donald and Dorothy Fairley

The Hand on My Scalpel
Humorous & Heartwarming Stories from a
Jungle Operating Room